Fabrics, Filth and Fairy Tents

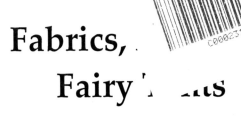

The Yorkshire Textile Districts in 1849

Angus Bethune Reach,
ed. Chris Aspin

Published by Royd Press
The Book Case
29 Market Street
Hebden Bridge
West Yorks.
HX7 6EU
www.bookcase.co.uk

First published by Helmshore Local History Society,
1973

This Royd Press edition, 2007

We apologise in advance for any unintentional
omissions or errors, which we will be happy to correct in
future editions.

ISBN: 978-0-9556204-0-9

CONTENTS

Introduction   1

Huddersfield and Dewsbury   3

Halifax and Bradford   25

Leeds   54

ILLUSTRATIONS

Cover illustrations: details from "The Industrial Aspect of Leeds from Richmond Hill" from *The Leeds Graphic,* 18th July 1885, lent by Chris Aspin.

Page 21: Photograph of Rag Merchants' Houses, 20-22 Station Road, Batley. By permission of English Heritage. NMR

Page 32: Photograph of aerial view of Shaw Lodge Mills lent by David Holdsworth of John Holdsworth & Co., Halifax

Page 66: Artist's impression of the "fairy tent" glass cupolas on Marshall's roof. By permission of English Heritage. NMR. More realistic views can be seen on the Leodis online photographic archive, www.leodis.net

Page 103: Briggate 1849, looking north to the entrance of Briggate and the old Leeds Bridge, with barges on the river. Engraver, T. A. Prior: Leeds Library and Information Services.

INTRODUCTION

IN October 1849, the *Morning Chronicle* began an investigation into the condition of the British working classes on a scale which no other newspaper had previously attempted or was ever to attempt again. Special correspondents visited all parts of the country, but apart from the London reports, which were written by Henry Mayhew, the project has been almost forgotten.[1] The correspondent chosen to describe the manufacturing districts of the North was Angus Bethune Reach (pronounced Re-ach), a young Scotsman of enormous energy, whose fluent and perceptive accounts of living and working conditions form one of the most impressive achievements of Victorian journalism. Reach began his investigations in Manchester and the surrounding textile towns[2] after which he spent a fortnight visiting the main centres of the Yorkshire textile industry. The *Morning Chronicle* carried Reach's letters on December 3 (Huddersfield and Dewsbury), December 6 (Halifax and Bradford), December 10 and 13 (Leeds).

---

[1] The survey was the starting point of Mayhew's *London Labour and London Poor*. Mayhew continued his investigations after leaving the *Morning Chronicle*.

[2] A. B. Reach, *Manchester and the Textile Districts in 1849*, (ed. C. Aspin), Helmshore, 1972. C.A. Helmshore, 1973.

The national survey - it appeared under the general heading " Labour and the Poor " - was prompted by the severe outbreak of cholera which focused attention on the condition of working people. "No man of feeling or reflection," said the newspaper in its introduction to the investigation, "can look abroad without being shocked and startled by the sight of enormous wealth and unbounded luxury placed in direct juxtaposition with the lowest extremes of indigence and privation. Is this contrast a necessary result of the unalterable laws of nature, or simply the sure indication of an effete social system?"

In trying to find the answer, the *Morning Chronicle* certainly succeeded, as it predicted it would, "in making very valuable additions to the general stock of knowledge", and today the numerous articles are a rich source of information for both the local and national historian. They deserve to be much better known.

Chris Aspin

Publisher's note: Reach's dense Victorian paragraphs can appear a bit daunting to the modern reader. For this edition, they have been broken down into sub-paras. His original paragraphs are marked with a line space.

HUDDERSFIELD AND DEWSBURY

THE town of Huddersfield is a species of minor capital of the board and fancy cloth working districts of Yorkshire - Leeds being taken as the general manufacturing metropolis of the county. In Huddersfield and its neighbourhood, however, a very important proportion of the cloth working of the entire district is carried on, and much of the fine-textured stuffs, conventionally known as "West of England goods", is spun, woven and finished on the banks of the Colne.

The township of Huddersfield contains rather more than 36,000, and the district comprehended by the Huddersfield Union is peopled by somewhat more than 108,000 inhabitants. The number of paupers at present accommodated in the several workhouses of the Union amounts to about 250, and the amount of out-door relief granted during a single week in the beginning of the present month was £186. In the year 1846, out of 939 couples who married 378 men and 696 women signed the register with their marks.

The value of life in Huddersfield, as stated in the Registrar's General Report, is 1 in 49 as regards males, and 1 in 52 as regards females; showing a degree of mortality less by nearly 10 per cent than that of Chorley, the healthiest of the cotton towns.

The population of Huddersfield and the surrounding districts are almost entirely engaged in the manufacture of wool - the scattered cotton and silk spinning and weaving establishments which may be found here and there being merely exceptions to the general rule. By far the greater part of the woollen manufacture of Huddersfield is carried on, in all its stages, in the mills. When weaving is put out, the work is generally executed by country people living within a circuit of some half dozen miles.

The species of fabric so manufactured is commonly that distinguished, in its different kinds, as fancy goods. The Ten Hours Bill applies to woollen factories just as it does to cotton mills. In the woollen districts, however, there seems to have been no attempt made to get rid of its restrictions. No mill, so far as my inquiries have extended, has sought to work by means of the relay system; and in the vast majority of instances, at least so far as regards the woollen in opposition to the worsted trade, no children are employed until they are above thirteen years of age.

The town of Huddersfield belongs to one ground landlord - Sir John Marsden. No building leases are granted, and the inhabitants are therefore, pro tanto, tenants at will. The town has sprung up almost entirely within the last sixty years. Previous to that time it was but an insignificant cluster of irregularly built lanes. The small manufacturers around brought in their wares upon pack horses and on the market-day exposed them for sale on the churchyard-wall. When the Cloth Hall was opened, many of these humble producers had not sufficient capital to rent a stall.

Although thus comparatively a new town, Huddersfield is by no means a well-built town. The houses inhabited by the working classes have, until very recently, been constructed back to back, or rather as double houses, a partition running from the ridge of the roof perpendicularly downwards.

The consequence of this system is that the more humble portions of the town - that is to say, three-fourths of it - are either exceedingly deficient in necessary conveniences, or the structures in question are erected in front of rows of houses, in positions perfectly destructive of anything like decent or seemly reserve.

A local act has, however, been lately obtained, applying to Huddersfield the provisions of one of the Health of Town Bills, and under this act the borough commissioners are proceeding with energy and vigour to remedy, so far as they can effect it, the sanitary grievances of the township. A scheme is in agitation for the opening up of an important continuation of the main street, and it is hoped that in the construction of the new quarter which will thus spring into being, proper sanitary regulations will be observed.

The processes of converting wool into broad cloth or fancy goods are carried on both in and out of the mills, but the strong tendency of the trade is to concentrate itself in the factories under the eyes of the proprietors, who very generally complain of the dilatoriness of the home workmen and the uncertainty of their completing their tasks by the stipulated time. The workpeople, on the other hand, maintain that they suffer from the caprice of the employers in bestowing work, and from the frequency with which they are compelled to make repeated journeys to the warehouses or mills before they obtain the yarn which they are to spin and weave in their own homes.

The houses inhabited by the factory hands of Huddersfield consist in most cases of a large parlour-kitchen opening from the streets, with a cellar beneath it, and either two small bedrooms or one large one above. In some instances a scullery is added to the main apartment. The general style of furniture is much the same as that which distinguishes the operative dwellings of the cotton district.[1] If there be any difference, I should say that that of Huddersfield seems the more plainly substantial of the two. The clock and the corner cupboards and the shelves glittering with ranges of dishes and plates are to be found as universally as in Manchester, and a plentiful supply of good water is in general conducted into every house.

Taking wages as the test of social condition, the operatives of Huddersfield may be considered as very fairly situated. Children below thirteen years of age are seldom employed in the mills, and the average earnings of those over that age may be 5s. weekly. The earnings of the women may vary from 7s. or thereabouts - obtained by those who pick and boil - to 9s. or 10s. or thereabouts, obtained by those who weave. The average may be about 8s. 6d. The average wage of the women is raised by the number of their sex who work at the loom, as the average wage of the men is depressed by the same cause. Slubbers, carders, spinners, dyers, fullers, raisers, and finishers may average about 18s. a week. Taking into account the number of adult males employed as weavers, both by power and hand, the general average sinks, and may be placed at from 14s. to 15s. per week.

Admitting these estimates to be generally correct, the average wage earned by adults in Huddersfield may be placed at 11s. 6d. a week - an amount very similar to the general run of wages in the cotton districts, while the average earned by all sexes and ages may be estimated at

---

[1] See A. B. Reach, *Manchester and the textile districts* in 1849, Helmshore, 1972, *passim.*

something more than 9s. I have said that the Huddersfield cottage houses are generally constructed back to back, and that a common arrangement is their division into a cellar or store place, a kitchen-parlour, and a large bedroom above it. The rents paid range from £7 to £8, or about 3s. per week.

The yarns given out by the mills to be spun and woven at the homes of the workpeople are taken to the rural districts around, or to the remote suburbs of Huddersfield. At a little village called Paddock, about a mile from the town, a number of looms are generally going. Proceeding there, I entered upon a series of domiciliary visits. The general arrangements of the houses were similar. The rooms invariably occupied the first floor. In some cases one and two uncurtained beds, almost invariably left unmade, were placed in corners. In other instances, the sleeping arrangements were upon the ground floor, or within a third chamber roughly partitioned off from the first apartment.

In the first house I entered, one loom only was at work. The weaver was manufacturing a rough greyish cloth for a peculiar sort of great coat. It was a web by which he could earn 17s. a week. He had not always so good a job, and with his wife to wind for him, he did not on the average earn so much as 10s. a week.

There were four in the family - his wife, himself, and two children, too young as yet to be of any use to their parents. In answer to my inquiries as to what they lived upon, the weaver said that as dinner must now be almost ready, I had better go below and satisfy myself. I did so, and found that the fare for the family consisted of two huge pig's pettitoes, with bread and potatoes. The weaver's wife said that dear times "was always a candle that burned at both ends with them", for when bread, potatoes, and meal was at the dearest, work was always the scarcest.

"Aye," said her husband, who had in the meantime descended to dinner, "we've found that oot long ago."

In another house I found that only two people resided, a man and his wife. They had no family. The bedroom was, in this instance, partitioned off from the loom room. It was carpeted with a strip of drugget, and looked decent, if not comfortable. There were two looms here for the husband and wife.

The man, who was busy, stopped his shuttle to speak to me. For the cloth which he was weaving he could have got seven years ago 10d. a yard -the price now paid was only 4½d. When he had pretty regular work his average weekly earnings were about 10s. For this he frequently worked from six o'clock in the morning until eight o'clock at night. Last summer trade had been bad with him, and one week with another he had not much above 3s. The earnings of his wife generally amounted to about 3s. 6d. per week. Taking an average, he thought that their united earnings might be about 12s. 6d. or 13s. a week. This was when trade was tolerably good. Sometimes they could not make more than 10s. a week between them. He paid for his house £8 10s. per annum. The poor rates were 6d. 3d., the highway rates 3s. 2½d., and the charge for water, 5s. The woollen hand-loom weavers about Huddersfield were very ill off.

"If they have young families," said the woman, "that is, families over young to help them by working in the mills, they don't get half enough to eat."

"It was not often, however, that the mills would take the children until they were thirteen years of age, and legally able to work ten hours a day. They might then earn from 5s. to 6s. a week as piecers."

I told the weaver that I had heard a great deal about slack work and dear food coming together in this trade, and asked him if he had ever noticed anything of the kind.

"It would be queer, indeed, if I hadn't done that," he said. "We had a long spell of high prices since 1846, and I'll tell you what was the consequence to me. For sixteen months I had only four webs, at 34s. a piece. Not a bit of work more than that came into this house."

"Why," I said, " did you live upon £6 16s. for near a year and a half?" "We did, sir. God knows how- -but somehow we did; and flour was then 4s. a stone. The flour you can get now for 1s. 11d."

"I don't call it living," said the wife. "We kept ourselves alive, but that was all."

There are a considerable number of "low Irish" in Huddersfield, but the effect of the sanitary reform measures in process of being carried out, is to drive them forth from the borough into the adjacent townships, where they cannot be hindered from pigging together on the floors of garrets and cellars by dozens and scores. The sanitary act applied to Huddersfield gives the local board of works power to regulate the number of persons to be accommodated in each common lodging-house, and, as a consequence, the Irish population within the borough is rapidly diminishing.

I paid a visit to several of their haunts - these being principally the uncleansed alleys and fever-smelling *cul-de-sacs* in the higher parts of the town.

The first domicile which - accompanied by Mr. Joshua Hobson, the very efficient and courteous clerk to the Board of Works - I visited had been a lodging-house, and only been very recently cleared out. The occupants of the two rooms of which it consisted were an old woman, her two daughters, and a tolerably numerous array of grandchildren. In a corner of the lower room, a flock bed with a dirty rug was rolled up. The grandmother slept here. When the place had been a lodging-house she slept down in the cellar.

We descended the stairs to inspect the dormitory. It was lightless and airless - the earthen floor and stone walls were sopping with foetid damp, and the smell clearly showed that the place was used as a cesspool as well as a cellar. In this noisome hole the family kept their supply of drinking water.

The bed-room above the common apartment might measure about 16 feet by 12 feet. It contained two beds - mere frames covered with brown rugs, which lay in wisps just as the occupants of the couches had left them. In this room, when the dwelling was used as a lodging-house, upwards of twenty people were accustomed to sleep, huddled together upon rags flung on the floor.

The common room was furnished with a few coarse household articles, lying littered about in squalid disorder. Broken plates, dirty knives, forks, pewter spoons, and such like were scattered on tables, chairs, and the filth-encrusted floor; and amongst them was piled a heap of frowsy smelling rags, mouldy bones, old iron and empty medicine phials, the produce of the last day's excursion of the landlady of the domicile. I could wring little from her as to the ordinary profits of her trade as a rag collector. She had been prevented from keeping the swarm of lodgers which her house had formerly accommodated, and seemed to be exceedingly sore upon that, and indeed upon most other subjects.

The next house we entered was also rented by a woman. Her husband had gone to America, and she expected that he would shortly send money for her to go out and join him. In the meantime she was principally supported by his remittances, and by taking in lodgers at as many pence a night as they could afford to give her.

The house, although it was tenanted by two almost idle women - the landlady and her sister - was in a slatternly state of filthiness, the rickety furniture scattered about the room – the dirty children roaring on the floor - broken crockery containing the heads and tails of rank-smelling herrings, the fragments of breakfast, left unheeded on the table and chair – and the single window a mass of dust and mud stains.

Neither of the women of the house had any particular occupation. They stowed away what lodgers they could get, and vegetated on from day to day in the midst of filth and stenches, the major part of which a forenoon's work would remove.

Next door to this place was a cellar-dwelling. Access to the apartment - if it can be called one - had formerly been obtained by means of a flight of stairs from the ground floor of the house above; but these had been blocked up, and as there was a small sunken area on the outside, an extra door, or rather hole, not four feet high, had been broken in the wall, and through this the inmates crawled backwards and forwards. This den - the place was about eight feet by six – was inhabited by a man, his wife, and several children.

The man was a mason's labourer, and in constant work, earning 14s. per week. The woman did the house work, as she said. Filthy plates, and tubs full of foul-smelling scum and slops lying everywhere about, testified how diligently she performed her duties, which were rendered more onerous by the children of a neighbour being committed to her care, while the mother was absent upon a country expedition, exchanging pots and pans against old iron, glass, bones, and rags. For taking charge of the children in question the woman received from their mother fourpence a day.

While we were talking, a stout built fellow, the model of a stalwart navvy, lounged into the cellar and seated himself on the window sill. This man seemed a perfect specimen of good natured laziness. He worked, he said, when he got a job. He could then make 15s. a week, but there wasn't much doing in his way at present. His wife was out gathering rags and bones. I asked him whether he could not get work in any of the factories? He burst into a loudish good-natured laugh as he replied, "Bedad, sir, and is it me fingers yer would like to see snipped off entirely by them blissid machinery. Sure I can handle a hoe or a pick; but them mules and looms is a pig with another snout entirely."

I was anxious to ascertain the particulars of the pot and rag trade, by which so many of the Huddersfield Irish live, and after some trouble and much collation of the facts deposed to by the gathers, with those affirmed by the rag merchants, ascertained that the business is usually conducted as follows:

The rag-gather comes in the morning to the rag-merchant's shop, and obtains a number of coarse earthenware pots, pans, and pipkins upon credit. With these he or she sets out on the expedition, very often making a circuit of more than a score of miles - offering at every promising house the earthenware in exchange for rags, white or coloured, bones or old glass.

The products of the swapping is brought to the rag-merchant, who gives about 1½d. per lb. for white rags, from 6d. to 7d. per stone for coloured rags, and 4d. per stone for old iron. The day's transactions are then settled between the rag-collector and the rag-buyer, the latter paying the former the balance produced by the value of the rags, offal, etc., over the value of the pots. Sometimes, on very lucky days, the balance amounts to 1s. 6d. A very few pence, however, more frequently settles the account; and it is not very uncommon for the balance to be - for the rag-collector - on the wrong side of the book altogether. The number of English who pursue this traffic is inconsiderable, and they seldom or never make the lengthened circuits which the Irish are in the daily habit of traversing. Many of the latter hawk salt about, with tapes, staylaces, buttons, and all the usual *et ceteras* of cadging pedlars.

"Och, indeed, sir," said a woman to me, "it's a hard life intirely. Sure you may walk till you're foot-sore, and after, and knock at twenty doors before you knock the value of a brass farden out of any of them."

In one of the courts of one of the Irish quarters - a place, by the way, reeking with abominations, but which the authorities are energetically improving - I observed one house, poor indeed in appearance, but notably clean. On entering it I found that the inhabitants were English, the only English people in the court. They had lived there for more than thirty years, and always paid their way. I found them, however, in deep poverty, and their story was affecting. The family consisted of five - an old man, his old wife, their daughter, her husband, and the infant of the latter couple. The grandfather had worked all his life in a woollen mill, but he was now, in the estimation of the masters, too old to be employed. He had gone from mill to mill in Huddersfield, begging in vain for work. His wife was quite past all labour, and the family were entirely supported by the daughter's husband, whose earnings amounted only to 13s, a week.

The old man, the woman said, was wearing himself away fretting at the idea of being a burden upon the husband of his daughter. The latter was to go into a mill the moment the infant could be left with its grandmother. "It was cruel," she said, speaking of her husband and struggling to keep back her tears, "to see a hearty man trying to work hard day after day on nothing but bread and a little milk." The contrast between this poor family and their lazy Irish neighbours was very striking and very painful.

The Huddersfield Mechanics' Institution is, out of all sight, the best conducted and most useful establishment of the kind I have seen in the north of England. In too many towns, the mechanics' institute really means a cheap news-room, with an occasional trashy concert for the subscribers.

In Huddersfield the case is very different. The Mechanics' Institution there is a vigorously working and most effective educational establishment, supported not so much by occasional galas, and factitious and incidental contributions, as by the steady assistance of a large body of working men. The names upon the books, as fortnightly and quarterly subscribers, are about 1,000; and since 1844, upwards of 2,860 persons have partaken of the advantages of the institution.

I was surprised and delighted when conducted through the establishment and shown the great number of young men diligently and methodically pursuing different courses of study. In one room, the members were engaged in constructing maps, the drawing roughly executed to be sure, but zeal and intelligence everywhere most strikingly manifest.

There exists, in connection with the institution, a school of design, very efficiently superintended, in which I found about twenty pupils of every age from 12 to 40, but all of them of the working class, busily employed in drawing from the antique. On another night in the week the class meets for instruction in mechanical art. Altogether, the Huddersfield Mechanics' Institute is a model which may be most advantageously studied by many similar establishments of much greater pretensions and much smaller performance.

The small town of Dewsbury holds, in the woollen district, very much the same position which Oldham does in the cotton country. The reader will remember that an essential feature in the manufacture of the latter town is the spinning and preparing of waste and refuse cotton.[1] To this stuff the name of shoddy is given, but the real and orthodox shoddy is a production of the woollen districts, and consists of the second-hand wool manufactured by the tearing up, or rather the grinding, of woollen rags by means of coarse willows, called devils; the operation of which sends forth choking clouds of dry pungent dirt and floating fibres – the real and original "devil's dust". Having been, by the agency of the machinery in question, reduced to something like the original raw material, fresh wool is added to the pulp in different proportions, according to the quality of the stuff to be manufactured, and the mingled material is at length re-worked in the usual way into a coarse and little serviceable cloth.

There are some shoddy mills in the neighbourhood of Huddersfield, but the mean little town of Dewsbury may be taken as the metropolis of the manufacture, and thither I accordingly proceeded.

The first mill I visited was that belonging to the Messrs. Blakely, in the immediate outskirts of the town. This establishment is devoted solely to the sorting, preparing, and grinding of rags, which are worked up in the neighbouring factories. Great bales choke full of filthy tatters lay scattered about the yard, and loaded waggons were fast arriving and adding to the heap.

As for the mill, a glance at its exterior showed its character. It being a calm, still day, the walls and part of the roof were covered with the thick clinging dust and fibre, which ascended in choky volumes from the open doors and glassless windows of the ground floor, and

---

[1] See A. B. Reach, *Manchester and the textile districts in 1849,* Helmshore, 1972, pp. 79-83.

which also poured forth from a chimney, constructed for the purpose, exactly like smoke. On a windy day I was told that the appearance of the place would be by no means so bad, as a thorough draft would carry the dust rapidly away to leeward. As it was, however, the mill was covered as with a mildewy fungus, and upon the grey slates of the roof the frowzy deposit could not be less than two inches in depth.

We went first into the upper story, where the rags are stored. A great wareroom was piled in many places from the floor to the ceiling with bales of woollen rags, torn strips and tatters of every colour peeping out from the bursting depositaries.

There is hardly a country in Europe which does not contribute its quota of material to the shoddy manufacturers. Rags are brought from France, Germany, and in great quantities from Belgium. Denmark, I understand, is favourably looked upon by the tatter merchants, being fertile in morsels of clothing, of fair quality. Of domestic rags, the Scotch bear off the palm; and possibly no one will be surprised to hear, that of all rags, Irish rags are the most worn, the filthiest, and generally the most unprofitable.

The gradations of value in the world of rags are indeed remarkable. I was shown rags worth £30 per ton, and rags worth only 30s. The best class is formed of the remains of fine cloth the produce of which, eked out with a few bundles of fresh wool, is destined, as broad cloth, or at all events as pilot cloth, to go forth to the world again. Fragments of damask and skirts of merino dresses formed the staple of middle class rags; and even the very worst bales - to my eye they appeared unmitigated masses of frowzy filth - afford here and there some fragments of calico, which are wrought up into brown paper. The refuse of all mixed with the stuff which even the shoddy-making devil rejects, is packed off to the agricultural districts for use as manure. I saw several unpleasant smelling lots which were destined to fertilise the hop-gardens of Kent.

Under the rag ware-room was the sorting and picking area. Here the bales are opened, and their contents piled in close, poverty-smelling masses upon the floor. The operatives were entirely women. They sat upon low stools, or half sunk and half enthroned amid heaps of filthy goods, busily employed in arranging them according to the colour and the quality of the morsels, and from the more pretending quality of rags carefully ripping out every particle of cotton which they could detect. Piles of rags of different sorts, dozens of feet high, were the obvious fruits of their labour.

All the women were over eighteen years of age, and the wages which they were paid for ten hours' work were 6s. per week. They looked squalid and dirty enough, but all of them were chattering, and several singing, over their noisome labour. The atmosphere of the room was close and oppressive; and although I perceived no particularly offensive smell, we could not help being sensible of the presence of a choky, mildewy sort of odour – a hot, moist exhalation - arising from the sodden smouldering piles as the workwomen tossed armfuls of rags from one heap to another. In this mill, and at this species of work - the lowest and foulest which any phase of the factory system can show - I found, for the first time, labouring as regular mill hands, Irish women.

The devils were, as I have said, upon the ground floor. The choking dust burst out from door and window, and it was not until a minute or so that I could see the workmen, moving amid the clouds catching up armfuls of the sorted rags and tossing them into the machine to be torn into fibry fragments by the whirling revolutions of its spiky teeth.

So far as I could make out, the place was a large bare room- the uncovered beams above, the rough stone walls, and the woodwork of the unglazed windows being as it were furred over with clinging woolly matter. On the floor, the dust and coarse filaments lay as if, to use the quaint phrase of a gentleman present, "it had been snowing snuff". The workmen were of course coated with the flying powder. They wore bandages over their mouths, so as to prevent as much as possible the inhalation of the dust, and seemed loath to remove the protection, for a moment.

Not one of them, however, would admit that he found the trade injurious. No, the dust tickled them a little, that was all. They felt it most of a Monday morning after being all Sunday in the fresh air. When they first took to the work it hurt their throats a little, but they drank mint tea and that soon cured them.

I asked whether there was not a disorder known as "shoddy fever"? The reply was, that they were all more or less subject to it, especially after tenting the grinding of the very dusty sorts of stuff - worsted stockings, for example. The "shoddy fever" was a sort of stuffing of the head and nose, with sore throat, and it sometimes forced them to give over work for two or three days, or at most a week; but the disorder, they said, was not fatal, and left no particularly bad effects. This was the statement, generally corroborated, of a person who had worked for years in the horrible atmosphere which I have described.

In another mill two Irish women who fed the devils told me that they had been working there, one sixteen and the other eighteen months, and had experienced no perceptible change in their health.

In spite of all this, however, it is manifestly impossible for human lungs to breathe under such circumstances without suffering. I myself was exposed to the atmosphere in several mills for perhaps ten minutes altogether, and the experiment left an unpleasant. choky sensation in the throat, which lasted all the remainder of the day.

An intelligent woman in Batley Car, a village near Dewsbury, told me that the rag grinders were very subject to asthmatic complaints, particularly when the air was dull and warm. According to her, the shoddy fever was like a bad cold, with constant acrid running from the nose, and a great deal of expectoration. It was when there was a particularly dirty lot of rags to be ground that the people were usually attacked in this way, but the fever seldom kept them more than two or three days from their work.

In Batley I went over two shoddy establishments - the Bridge Mill and the Albion Mill. In both of these rags were not only ground, but the shoddy was worked up into coarse bad cloth, a great proportion of which is sent to America for slave clothing.

In one of the mills in question, the two rag grinders at work were the Irishwomen whom I have mentioned. They laboured in a sort of half roofed outhouse, the floor littered with rags and heaped with dust, the walls and beams furred with wavy down-like masses of filament, as though they had been inbedded in clusters of cobwebs, while the air, stirred by the revolving cylinders and straps, was a perfect whirlwind of pungent titillating powder.

Through this the women, with their squalid, dust-strewn garments, powdered to a dull greyish hue, and with their bandages tied over the greater part of their faces, moved like reanimated mummies in their swathings; I had seldom seen anything more ghastly.

The wages of these poor creatures do not exceed 7s. or 8s. a week. The men are much better paid, none of them making less than 18s. a week, and many earning as much as 22s. As I have mentioned, the amount of dust produced is different with different classes of rags. I may add, that when the better sort of material is consigned to the teeth of the "devil", a quantity of coarse rank oil which is thrown upon it, so as to cause the fibres to adhere better in the slubbing process, effectually lays the dust. There is no objection to the use of this oil, as I understand, in the grinding of any species of rags always excepting the expense.

After the rags have been devilled into shoddy, the remaining processes are much the same, although conducted in a coarser way, as those which I have already detailed in my description of the manufacture of woollen cloth. The wages hereabouts run, I am assured, quite as high as in the neighbourhood of Huddersfield, and some classes of workmen earn still more.

Dinner time came round when I was in one of the mills, and as many of the people had their meals carried to them, I had a good opportunity of observing the general style of the fare. Meat pies, with thick under-baked crusts, appeared to be the staple dish. The meal was despatched in the most primitive style. I observed one women helping herself to potatoes with one of the broad-bladed shears used for cutting rags.

The weaving is, for the most part, carried on at the homes of the workpeople. I visited several at Batley Car. The domestic arrangements consisted, in every case, of two tolerably large rooms, one above the other, with a cellar beneath - a plan of construction called in Yorkshire a " house and a chamber". The chamber had generally a bed amid the looms. The weavers were, as usual, complaining of irregular work and diminished wages.

Their average pay, one week with another, with their wives to wind for them – i.e., to place the thread upon the bobbin which goes into the shuttle – is hardly as much as 10s. a week. They work long hours, often fourteen per day. In one or two instances I found the weaver a small capitalist with perhaps half a dozen looms, and a hand-jenny for spinning thread, the workpeople being within his own family as regular apprentices and journeymen.

On my return to Dewsbury I applied to Dr. Hemingway, a gentleman who had a large practice in the district, for some precise information touching the "shoddy fever". The substance of the statement which I received is as follows:

The disease popularly known as "shoddy fever", and which is of too frequent occurrence hereabouts, is a species of bronchitis, caused by the irritating effect of the floating particles of dust upon the mucous membrane of the trachea and its ramifications. In general, the attack is easily cured particularly if the patient has not been for any length of time exposed to the exciting cause - by effervescing saline draughts to allay the symphtomatic febrile action, followed by expectorants to relieve the mucous membrane of the irritating dust; but a long continuance of employment in the contaminated atmosphere, bringing on as it does repeated attacks of the disease, is too, apt, in the end, to undermine the constitution, and produce a train of pectoral diseases, often closing with pulmonary consumption.

The doctor added, that ophthalmic attacks were by no means uncommon among the shoddy grinders, some of whom, however, wore wire gauze spectacles to protect the eyes. As regards the effect of the occupation upon health, Dr. Hemingway is of the opinion that, on a rough average, it may shorten life by about five years, taking of course, as the point of comparison, the average longevity of the district.

"Shoddy fever" is, in fact, a modification of the very fatal disease induced by what is called "dry grinding" at Sheffield; but of course the particles of woollen filaments are less fatal in their influence than the floating steel dust produced by the operation in question. The value of life in the Dewsbury district is about 1 in 47. It is always to be distinctly understood that the rag grinders constitute an exceedingly trifling minority of the workpeople employed. The operations which succeed that in which the devil plays the most important part, seem to be just as healthy as in those mills which prepare from the finer wools the finer cloth.

HALIFAX AND BRADFORD

THE manufacture of long-fibred wool differs from that of short-fibred wool in almost as many and as important respects as the general wool manufacture differs from the general cotton manufacture.

From the short-stapled wool are wrought all kinds of cloths - properly so called - and all the tribe of the warm fleecy stuffs, from winter shawls to blankets.

The long-stapled fleeces form the raw material of what is technically known as the "stuff" or "worsted" trade. To this branch of industry we are indebted for the twilled and untwilled fabrics, which may, for the convenience of the general reader, be described as belonging to the merino family. Strictly speaking, the latter term is applied only to stuffs twilled on both sides. Coburgs and Paramattas are twilled on one side, and moussline de laines and Orleans stuffs are untwilled. This twilling process is a technical peculiarity in the weaving, with which I have nothing to do.

All the fabrics which I have enumerated belong to the same industrial family, are manufactured out of the same general class of long-stapled fleeces; and (still speaking in a general way) at the same places and by the same stages of manufacture. The classes of "stuff" fabrics indicated above are those principally used for female attire. To the list, however, I may add another group of fabrics, manufactured from the long-stapled wool, and which may be conveniently indicated as damasks and moreens.[1]

I should not have adverted to these details - belonging, as they do, rather to the technicalities of manufacture than to the social and physical condition of the manufacturer - but that some general knowledge of what a man makes, and how he makes it, seems indispensable if we would judge correctly of his social position and the circumstances of his daily life. Some such explanations are in this case the more necessary, inasmuch as I have a shrewd guess that there are thousands of well-educated and tolerably informed people who will very probably associate the idea of worsted with the single production of warm winter stockings.

The worsted or stuff manufacture is, therefore, a branch of the woollen trade carried on in different districts, and under different social conditions, from that branch of the same trade which gives us broadcloths and blankets. Nothing is more remarkable than the unknown influences which so often determine the flow of a particular branch of textile industry to a particular locality, and in no more striking instance is this mysterious tendency manifested than in the woollen trade - using the word in its general sense - of Yorkshire.

In Huddersfield and Dewsbury hardly an ounce of long-stapled wool is to be seen. In Halifax and Bradford hardly an ounce of short-stapled wool is manufactured.

---

[1] Damasks - twilled table linen with woven designs shown by reflection of light. Moreens - stout material for curtains etc.

Leeds is the general industrial metropolis of the county, yet Huddersfield boasts that it is attaching to itself, from the larger town, the finer sorts of broadcloth; and Bradford can point to dozens of masters and hundreds of workmen who have recently made their way from the banks of the Aire, and flung their capital and their industry into what is now indisputably the metropolis of the worsted trade in England.

Huddersfield and Bradford, therefore, each in its own way, contend that they are gradually absorbing very important proportions of the enterprise and industry of Leeds.

Such being the present state of matters - Halifax being an old worsted-weaving and Bradford a new worsted-weaving town - let me shortly allude to the features which, in the most marked manner, distinguish the process of "stuff" making from that of "cloth" making.

In each the wool is sorted, picked, and torn into easily yielding filaments by the whirling teeth of the "willow". In the cloth trade, the carding machine and the slubbing frame next play their parts.

At the commencement of these latter processes, the worsted manufacture parts company, and proceeds by different stages. After being willowed and crashed, instead of being consigned to the carding-machine, the material - at least in the case of 90 lbs. out of every 100 lbs. - is delivered to the wool comber, whose labour I shall, in its due place, describe.

I ought to add here, that there has been lately introduced a sort of card-roving machine, very much like that which is used in the cotton trade, and which tears the wool into filaments, then brushes it, by a jerking motion, from the last cylinder, and collects the broad cobweb-like tissue into lengthened "slivers", like those produced by the hand-combers. The coarser sorts of wool only, however, are as yet subjected to this process; and the impression is strong among the hand-combers that it will not, in any formidable degree, compete with their already poorly-paid industry.

The woollen slivers, or card rovings, have now to be drawn, and afterwards spun - the operations being, in principle, precisely those of the cotton manufacture. In the stuff manufacture, however, no mule, with its extended ranges of spindles, and its advancing and retiring motion, is used. The thread is spun upon stationary frames, somewhat in the same manner as silk, and the only adult male labour put in requisition for the process is that of superintendents or overlookers, each of whom may have a dozen of frames committed to his charge.

In the weaving department, the power-loom is used to a greater extent than in the manufacture of cloth; the nature of the threads - which, to some extent, are akin to cotton -determining the mode of manufacture. When "stuffs" are woven, they may - except, perhaps, for the operations of the dye-house - be considered as ready for sale, such fabrics not involving the multiform finishing processes necessary in the production of glossy broadcloth.

So much for the technical differences between the production of woollen cloths and stuffs. In these differences are involved matters tending to produce to a very considerable extent, different social phases amid the workpeople.

Stuff manufacture is a much cleaner trade than woollen manufacture. Stuff mills rival, if they do not surpass, silk mills in cleanliness, and coolness, and sweetness of atmosphere. The dye is rarely applied until the fabric is turned out of the factory. There is little or no oil used in, or evolved by the process. No high temperature is requisite, at least so far as the mills go; and altogether the work carried on in the stuff factories is well calculated to exhibit in the most favourable light the physical condition of the labourers.

Notwithstanding all this, however, the stuff manufacturers are worse off than the woollen manufacturers, when tried by the grand test of the labourer's condition - his wages. In the stuff-mills there are employed, at the very least, a score of women, boys and children to one man. The adult males employed at the machinery are either the few who are overlookers, or the rather larger number who are forced to compete with women and girls at the power-loom.

The great bulk of the male worsted population work at the unwholesome, easily-acquired, and miserably paid for - because easily learned - labour of wool-combing.

Thus the average of wages is kept lower than in the cotton and cloth, and about as low perhaps as in the silk districts.

The average wages of adult male workmen engaged in the stuff trade cannot be above 10s. a week, at the most liberal estimate.

That of women ranges closely up to them, for a female weaver will earn as much or more, than a male comber. And as for the children, the average of the wages which they receive is kept down by the great number of "half-timers" - boys and girls under thirteen years of age, who are employed. Exclusive of half-time workers and young persons, the average weekly wages of male and female adults may be reckoned as from 8s. 6d. to 9s. 6d. - lower by about 2s. 6d. than the average wages in the cotton districts, reckoning in both cases on a time of fair prosperity, and a period of ten hours daily toil.

Halifax and Bradford are, as I have said, the centres of the stuff manufacture. The former town possesses, however, other industrial resources than that of the staple trade.

The mayor, Mr. Crossley,[1] for instance, is the chief partner in an immense carpet manufacturing establishment, employing about 1,500 hands, principally adult males, and paying about £1,000 weekly in wages.

Besides this and other establishments of different kinds the worsted manufacturers of Halifax prepare so great a variety of the staple production that periods of distress fall in general lighter upon them than on their Bradford neighbours.

The latter town is, perhaps. more quickly and keenly affected by the variations of trade than any other manufacturing depot in England. The masters are generally reputed as bold speculators; and the millowner who ventures his money freely, hazards, of necessity, the wages of his people as well as his own profits.

In Halifax, however, things are conducted more slowly and quietly. Compared with Bradford, the

---

[1] Francis Crossley (1817-1872). The firm of J. Crossley & Sons, Dean Clough Mills, was the largest producer of carpets in the world.

place has a touch of antiquity in its aspect and its tone.

So far as appearance goes no two towns can be more dissimilar. Halifax is an ancient borough, girdled by an *enceint* of mills and mill-hands' dwellings. Bradford seems spick and span new from the centre to the circumference.

There are points in the town of Halifax, from which the gazer will be put in mind of the quaint cities of Normandy and Bavaria - Rouen or Bamberg - so steep and narrow are the streets, and so picturesque the plaster walls streaked with chequering beams of blackened wood - the numerous street-turned gables - the ledge-like stories, each overhanging the other - and the grey and time-tarnished hue of the great coarse slates which form the high crow-footed and ridgy roofs. There is a fine Norman church, rising, wan and weather-stained, from its field of graves; and an odd, old-fashioned, nondescript building, in the centre of the town, traditionally called the Castle, and from the battered pinnacles of which watchers were wont to guard the approaches to the borough - against what habitual foemen tradition does not seem to be by any means clear.

Mr. Smith, of Deanston, in a sanitary report made about 1837, describes Bradford as being the dirtiest town in England.[1] Mr. Smith must have

---

[1] Deanston's *Report on the Condition of the Town of Bradford* is included in the *Second Report of the Commissioners for inquiring into the state of large towns and populous districts, Vol. II, 1845.*

written ere he extended his researches to Halifax. At all events Bradford is rapidly improving. The corporation is busy paving and draining; but that of Halifax has as yet been able to do nothing.

I ought to add that both towns have received their municipal charters within the last two years, and that Halifax is now, or has been until very lately, unprovided with any funds to carry on a sanitary campaign. The sooner, however, that it begins, the better. Few towns in England are better situated for being effectually drained. Mainly placed on the side of a steepish hill, with a rapid stream running at the bottom, Halifax ought to be a miracle of cleanliness, instead of, as it is, a marvel of dirt. The state of the low back streets and of the dwellings which compose them, I shall presently sketch.

The first factory in Halifax which I visited was that of the Messrs. Holdsworth.[1] It is a vast establishment,

---

[1] John Holdsworth & Co., worsted spinners and manufacturers, Shaw Lodge Mills. Aerial view above.

weaving all manner of stuff goods, situated upon the outskirts of the town, and surrounded by the dwelling of the workpeople. The active and energetic chief of the firm conducted me through the works.

The weaving shed is one of the noblest structures of the kind I have ever seen, perfectly lighted, not only by ordinary windows, but by means of a species of serrated roof, the perpendicular portions of which are glass. That the arrangements for ventilation are excellent was sufficiently proved by the perfectly fresh state of the atmosphere, and the workpeople laboured with spirit and energy. There were a few jacquard looms in the shed, but the greater number were of the ordinary kind. There might have been about one man present to every ten women and girls. The wages of the former average 10s., those of the latter 8s. weekly.

In estimating the remuneration of workpeople, I am frequently puzzled to reconcile the statements of the operatives and those of their masters, and yet I believe both to be grounded on fact. Where the amount of wages fluctuates with the skill of the workman and the quality of the fabric wrought, two parties looking at the question from different points of view will almost invariably state results each of which is capable of being supported by figures representing the sums earned or the sums paid, but neither giving a really fair view of the case.

The master will frequently strike an average from what his best hands working at the best jobs may earn. The labourer will just as frequently base his calculations upon what the most ordinary hands working on the most ordinary jobs do receive.

In neither case can you complain of absolute want of truth, but in both cases you will have to lament an equal absence of candour. In visiting the homes of the poor, accompanied by relieving officers, I have been again and again cautioned by my guides not to accept as literal truth the statements which were made to me.

"All the class upon the confines of pauperism - the class which are in daily risk of becoming paupers - will understate their incomes purposely for me to hear, and will perhaps afterwards appeal to what I cannot deny that I heard them state."

This was the warning given by a most active, intelligent, and, as I believe, kind-hearted relieving officer in Bradford; and I think that I am bound to repeat it here. My only aim is to hit the truth. I shall give the statements made to me by labourers and masters, guarded by the rules of belief which I have myself been able to educe, as well as by the caution of non-interested parties.

To return to the workpeople of Messrs. Holdsworth's factory. The vast majority of weavers were young women. In neatness and propriety of dress they rivalled the silk spinners and shawls and bonnets were hung along the walls, as I have described them in Macclesfield.[1]

In a smaller spinning room. the machinery ran quicker - so quickly, indeed, as to cause a perceptible tremor in the building, and here the wages of the workwomen ranged somewhat higher. To be removed to

---

[1] For Reach's account of Macclesfield, see *Manchester and the Textile Districts in 1849*, Helmshore, 1972, pp. 88-96.

the quick spinning room was to be promoted. In the carding, drawing, and spinning departments, the mechanism was almost exclusively looked after by women and girls, at the low wages of 5s. and 5s. 6d. The men employed were overlookers, and earned from 15s. to 22s. The ventilation in these rooms was hardly so good as in the weaving shed, but still I cannot say that there was much to complain of.

The girls looked hale and hearty, and Mr. Holdsworth was energetic in calling my attention to their plumpness, a quality which in a large majority of cases they certainly possessed to a very fair degree.

The dinner hour arrived during our inspection. As a considerable proportion of women live too far from the mill to go home to their meal, arrangements are made for enabling them to take it upon the spot. A sort of small cookshop is established near the furnace of one of the steam engines, and thither every girl who pleases brings her dinner, ready cooked, but disposed in a dish so as to allow it to be readily warmed up again.

I stationed myself in the dinner-bar at noon, and so had an opportunity of seeing nearly 300 of the messes prepared, and they were handed out through a sort of buttery-hatch to each applicant as she shouted the number of her carding-machine, her spinning-frame, or her loom. The dinners consisted almost invariably of a portion of baked meat with potatoes, and in a few instances mushrooms. A great number had coffee and tea in little tin flagons. Altogether the dinners seemed substantial and nourishing. I was gratified by the appearance both of the consumers and the fare consumed.

Afterwards I visited, alone, the cottages of several of the workpeople connected with the mills. As a general rule the dwellings of the Lancashire operatives are better than those of their Yorkshire brethren. In the superior class of cotton-workers' houses you will find a parlour, a kitchen, and two bedrooms.

In Yorkshire the tenements are almost invariably double, and the equally constant rule of construction is a common room serving for parlour and kitchen, a cellar below, and a bed-chamber above. The Yorkshire apartments are perhaps larger than those of Lancashire, but the domestic conveniences afforded are very inferior.

The houses attached to the Messrs. Holdsworth's establishments are fair specimens of the ordinary construction throughout the towns of the county. Hearing that there were one or two hand-loom weavers manufacturing damasks in the place, I found out one of them.

The lower room was not absolutely squalid - but that is the best that can be said of it. Upstairs in the loom room was one of those unmade, brown frame-like beds, which I have so often seen. The weaver rated his average earnings from 8s. to 9s. With the best sort of work, and plenty of it, he could earn 15s., but the trade was dying out. His wages used to be double what they were now. The rent he paid was £5 a year.

I may observe that stuff handloom weaving seems likely to sink into the condition of cotton handloom weaving, the quality and tenseness of the threads of each fabric approaching each other pretty closely.

In the. other houses which I visited I found the furniture generally coarse, and sometimes scanty. The absence of convenient accommodation, so far as my experience goes, tends invariably to the production of household slovenliness. Give people a good house, and there is a far higher chance that they will become good housekeepers than if they live in a dwelling so constructed that they can take little pride in its accommodations or its arrangements.

Local acts are passed providing for the construction of tenements with free ventilation from the front to the back door.

From the Messrs. Holdsworth's mill I proceeded to another - that of Messrs. Ackroyd.[1] The average wages paid in this establishment were thus stated to me by a very intelligent overlooker. The adult males, not including the weavers, might have about 17s. a week. Female adults might average in the spinning and drawing rooms, about 6s. or 6s. 3d. Young persons, from 13 to 18, about 4s. 9d.; and children from 8 to 13, working five hours a day, from 1s. 9d. to 2s. 3d. In the weaving department my informant thought that the average rate earned by men and women might be somewhat above 8s. per week.

As in the case of the former mill, the factory in question was kept as clean as possible. It was dusk when I went through it - a period which may account for the atmosphere not feeling quite so fresh as did that of the last-mentioned establishment.

I have said that the streets of Halifax are disgracefully neglected. The remark applies especially to the courts and *culs de sac* inhabited by the very poor - including, of course, the Irish - and locally termed "foulds". I inspected several very closely, and found them reeking with stench and the worst sort of

---

[1] James Akroyd & Sons, worsted spinners, merchants and manufacturers, Bowling Dyke.

abomination. The ash-pits and appurtenances were disgustingly choked, ordure and filthy stagnant slops lay freely and deeply scattered around, often at the very thresholds of swarming dwellings - and among all this muck uncared-for children sprawled by the score, and idle slatternly women lounged by the half dozen.

The "low Irish" in Halifax are hawkers and rag collectors, like nearly all the brotherhood in the North of England. I talked to several in their cellars. One old woman, who had been more than thirty years in England, talked dolefully of the decline of the hawking trade. She had frequently, in her youth, she said, made 20s. out of one house. She carried about "chancy and such like". But the poor people now seldom earned more than a shilling, or eighteenpence at the very most, for a hard day's work.

This woman kept lodgings in a cellar. Two strapping fellows sat smoking by the smouldering fire. The beds were greasy mattresses partially covered with foul rags and rolled up in corners. In another cellar, which was almost totally dark, and for which its occupant paid 9d. a week, a grey-headed negro - an old man-of-war's man - had lived for seventeen years. He seldom or never stirred out - vegetating there in a world of dirt and darkness.

All the "foulds" which I penetrated were of the same class. The vilest filth lying unswept and seemingly unheeded - the most noxious stenches filling the air - the grimy houses and ordure-covered stones swarming with a foul, a lazy, and - worse than both - a seemingly contented population. The corporation of Halifax have a perfect Augean stable to clean. and the sooner they set about it the better for the health and character of their town.

Of course there are a great number of woolcombers in Halifax, but the account which I shall give of these workmen in Bradford will suffice for both.

Let us now proceed, then, to the latter place. In an architectural point of view, the best features of Bradford consist of numerous ranges of handsome warehouses. The streets have none of the old-fashioned picturesqueness of those of Halifax. The best of them are muddy, and not too often swept. Mills abound in great plenty, and their number is daily increasing, while the town itself extends in like proportion.

Bradford is, as I have said, essentially a new town. Half a century ago it was a mere cluster of huts; now the district of which it is the heart contains upwards of 132,000 inhabitants. The value of life is about 1 in 40. Fortunes have been made in Bradford with a rapidity almost unequalled even in the manufacturing districts. In half a dozen years men have risen from the loom to possess mills and villas.

At present, stuff manufacturers are daily pouring into the town from Leeds, while a vast proportion of the wool-combing of the empire seems, as it were, to have concentrated itself in Bradford. I was struck by the accent in which many of the woolcombers addressed me; and, in answer to my inquiries, I had frequently a roomful of workmen exclaiming,

"I'm from Leicestershire" - "I'm from Devonshire" - "I'm from Cornwall"   -"I'm from Mount Mellick, in Queen's County".

As I have hinted, the Bradford employers are, in the slang of the manufacturing districts, accounted "high-pressure men". I have been told that a mere spirit of rapid demand is sufficient to cause loom-shed after loom-shed to arise. The fabrics manufactured being also of the same general class, their sale increases and diminishes simultaneously, and the consequence is that every shade of variation in the market means hundreds of dinners the more or less in Bradford.

A town of this class is just one of those on which, in prosperous seasons, the flood of agricultural pauperism bears down. Trade is at present exceedingly brisk in Bradford - so brisk that even stables are put into requisition to contain the wool, for lack of warehouse room. The number of persons, therefore, receiving parish relief is comparatively small, and, excepting an isolated case or two, I am told that not a single native of the town is upon the books.

The paupers are mainly Irish and English agricultural labourers who have not as yet learned to be useful in their new sphere. In the last period of commercial stagnation, about two out of every five labourers in Bradford were out of employment. A test, consisting of shovelling and wheeling earth was established and about 1s. 6d. per head was weekly paid to all unable to find work. The revival of trade was marked by the most gratifying social tokens. The masters, following the example of the Mayor, gave either dinners or holidays, and railway trips, to all their hands. Upwards of £2,000 was thus expended during the last summer, and the addresses of thanks presented in all instances by the working hands were so worded as to afford gratifying proof of the good feeling between employer and employed.

With the exception of a few of the main thoroughfares, which are bustling, and characterised by good shops, and in many cases by the handsome ranges of warehouses which I have alluded to, Bradford may be described as an accumulation of mean streets, steep lanes, and huge mills intersected here and there by those odious patches of black, muddy, vast ground rooted up by pigs, and strewn with oyster-shells, cabbage-stalks, and such garbage, which I have so often noticed as commonly existing in manufacturing towns.

Since Mr. Smith, of Deanston, passed sentence upon Bradford, the corporation, although they might have done more, have not been idle. Upwards of thirty streets and lanes have been paved and drained, and some of the worst Irish colonies have been materially improved. I was taken to see one locality which had been the worst in Bradford, and which was once a constant well-spring of fever. It has been opened up, drained, paved, and regularly cleansed, and is now not fouler than an average dirty lane.

The houses of the workpeople are very inferior. They are one and all constructed back to back, or rather built double, with a partition running down from the ridge of the roof. This is the case even in rows and streets at present building.

"The plan," said my informant, "is adopted because of its cheapness, and because it saves ground rent."

Cellars are very numerous in Bradford, and not one operative family in a hundred possesses more than two rooms - "a house and a chamber".

In respect of dwelling accommodation, the worst feature of the stuff and woollen towns is that they seem to be making little or no progress. In the cases of ranges of houses, even of a comparatively superior class, the privies are built in clusters, in a small space, left open behind, instead of each being placed in a quiet, decent situation, close to the house to which it belongs.

Bradford, like Halifax, is well situated for drainage. There is ample fall, and the "Bradford Beck", a rapid stream which flows through the town, would, if arched over, make a capital main sewer. This brook at present runs the colour of ink. The relieving officer, with whom I inspected the town, showed me a spot where the foul water washed the grimy walls of half a dozen steaming mills.

"There," he said, "when I was a boy, I used to catch trout in as bright a stream as any in Yorkshire."

The two towns in England, indeed, which within the last half-century have sprung up most rapidly, form an odd pair. They are Brighton and Bradford.

We proceeded first to see some of the low Irish haunts. As usual, the great majority of the adults are hawkers, but a few of them are woolcombers. Of these I shall have something to say presently.

Rags, and in some cases brushes, form the staple of their trades. Instead of exchanging pots and mugs, the collectors frequently barter salt for rags, the terms being always pound for pound. Sevenpence a stone was the market value of mixed rags - sixpence a stone that of bones. The average earnings of the hawkers they stated as from 1s. to Is. 6d. a day.

The general appearance of their houses I have frequently sketched. They almost always consist of a single room - generally a cellar - a low, dark, foul-smelling place, with rough stools, and a broken table or so lying about; coarse crockery, either unwashed or full of dirty water; knives without handles, and forks with broken prongs; bits of loaves smeared over by dirty hands; bundles of rags, buckets of slops, and unmade beds huddled on the stone or earthen floor in corners.

There always seems to exist a sort of community of dwellings among these people, which I never find among their English neighbours. The doors invariably stand open, and when I inquire about the sleeping accommodation I am invariably told that half the people whom I find crouching round the fireplace smoking are only "naybours".

Sometimes I find a room almost empty, but before I am here a minute it is sure to be filled by the aforesaid naybours, who, having nothing to do, come stalking in to learn what my visit portends. In a lodging-house which I saw, there was bed room for 16, at 3d. each; that is to say, there were four frames, covered with rags and rugs, in the lower room, and the same accommodation in the higher. The single men slept by themselves. Married couples and single women occupied the other apartment jointly. There could not, when I called, have been less than a dozen men and women smoking round the fire.

In an adjacent cellar the scene was perfectly savage. The floor was earth, covered with splints of wood produced in match making. The articles of furniture were two - a rough wooden trestle, on which were placed a broken brown plate and some herring-bones - and a square box, like a small coffin, in which lay an infant. A woman, with a skin so foul that she might have passed for a negress, was squatted on the ground - and a litter, I cannot call them a group, of children burrowed about her.

The woman could barely talk English; yet she must have been more than a dozen years in the country, for the eldest boy, an urchin fully as old, told me that he had been born in Lincolnshire. In a corner lay a litter of brown rags - the family bed. The rent paid for this place was 8d. a week.

As I have stated, the greatest part of the labour of male adults through the worsted districts consists in combing wool. In Bradford I was told on good authority that there are about 15,000 woolcombers.

These men sometimes work singly, but more often three or four or five club together and labour in what is called a shop, generally consisting of the upper room or "chamber" over the lower room or "house".

Their wives and children assist them to a certain extent in the first and almost unskilled portions of the operations, but the whole process is rude and easily acquired. It consists of forcibly pulling the wool through metal combs or spikes of different lengths, and set five or six deep.

These combs must be kept at a high temperature, and consequently the central apparatus in a combing room is always a "fire pot", burning either coke, coals, or charcoal, and constructed so as to allow three, four, or five combs to be heated at it - the vessel being in these cases respectively called a "pot o' three", a "pot o' four", or a "pot o' five".

When coals are burned, the pot is a fixed apparatus like a stove, with a regular funnel to carry away the smoke. When charcoal is used the pot is a movable vessel, without a funnel, the noxious fumes too often spreading freely in the room.

Scattered through the chamber are frequently two or more poles or masts, to which the combs, after being heated, are firmly attached while the workman drags the wool through them until he has reduced it to a soft mass of filament - when he educes the substances as it were, draws it by skilful manipulation out of the compact lump into long semi-transparent "slivers", which, after certain minor operations, are returned to the factory to be subjected to the "drawing machines".

The general aspect of a combing-room may therefore be described as that of a bare chamber, heated to nearly 85 degrees. A round fire-pot stands in the centre; masses of wool are heaped about; and four or five men, in their shirt sleeves, are working busily.

The first wool-combing apartment which I entered contained five workmen. There was a coal fire-pot in the centre, with a regular communication with the chimney. The heat was great, but modified by the windows being left open. The entire house consisted of the working room, and a cooking, sitting, and sleeping room beneath. The rent was 1s. 9d. It belonged to one man, to whom the rest paid each 4d. weekly. For this the landlord provided the necessary fire. The arrangement of a common room has reference principally to economy in fuel.

The masters who give out the wool to be combed pay a certain amount, called "fire-brass", wherewith to provide the necessary fuel. The "fire-brass", when paid in money, is about 1½d. for every 24 lb. of wool. When charcoal is employed, it is usual, however, for the masters to give fuel instead of money.

The estimate of wool-combers' wages given by the five workmen in this room was, that they amounted, on an average, to 8s. or 8s. 6d. per week. In Halifax the chief labourer in a similar room said that some hands might occasionally earn 12s. a week, but for this they laboured, 15, 16, and 17 hours out of the 24. He put the average at about 9s. a week. This comber afterwards corrected his original statement so far as to add, that in the 12s. a week be included the earnings of the wife, who frequently "picked and handfulled" the wool.

Wool-combers' hours, are, I believe, proverbially long. The men in Bradford said they were sometimes forced to work most of the night. Low as their wages are, they were recently still lower; but since the arrival of trade in the district, the wool-combers have raised the amount of their remuneration upwards of 3s. by three successive strikes.

The combers have now to compete with machinery. Each machine will do about ten times the work of a hand labourer, but it employs several hands, two of whom get good wages. These machines are in general, however, only used for the coarsest work, and did not seem to excite any great apprehension among the workmen.

Wool-combing is the only branch of manufacturing industry which 1 have yet met with supporting a fair proportion of adult Irish males. A number of them have been bred to the employment at Mount Mellick, in Queen's County.

The mass of the woolcombers of Yorkshire includes natives of almost all the southern counties of England. One and all, they were loud in their denunciations of the accommodation provided for their labour. In the south the masters used to provide shops for the work. Here the men had to labour in their houses, and often to sleep in the room in which they toiled.

They put it to me, whether the hot air I was breathing was fit for human beings to sleep in.

"But the furnace, the 'pot', is extinguished at night," I said.

"Never," they replied, "from Monday morning till Saturday night. It is always left with a smouldering glow of fire. But they're much worse off than us, those who use charcoal."

In this I fully agreed, and started off to see a "charcoal pot". I had not far to go. In an adjacent street I lighted upon a man working at mohair over a charcoal stove. The pot was funnelless and uncovered, and the noxious fuel glowed with a subdued bluish light. I was not sensible of any odours, but an immediately commencing headache told that there was something atmospherically wrong.

The woolcomber was a gaunt, sickly-looking man. His wife entered the room when we were speaking, and joined in the conversation. He said that combing mohair was a bad work. Mohair was a desperate thing to float and cling. He had often to brush away the fibres as they gathered round his lips, but he knew that he breathed some of 'em. The wife said that the work made her husband sick, often and often. But it was regular, and what could they do?

The charcoal was a terribly bad thing, he knew that. Why did he not use coal? Why, because the master would not allow him. The master thought charcoal best for combing mohair. He got no "fire brass", only charcoal. Sometimes it was stronger like than other times. Then it made him sickish, and he would to go out into the air for a while.

He worked from six in the morning till ten at night. He knew it wasn't wholesome, but "what could he do?" There being a bed in the room I asked who slept in it.

"Some of the children."

They had seven; five of them slept in that bed.

"But, of course," I said, "you put out the charcoal?"

The reply was, "Well, not exactly; but there's only a spark or so left burning and the window's a little down."

"But surely your children suffer from such an atmosphere?"

"Well, yes. Some odd times there is one of our little ones comes down in the morning very sickish, but what can we do?'"

Three of this man's children worked in the mills, earning among them 12s. a week. One of them, the eldest girl, was ill with scrofulous sores on her legs, for the cure of which the poor creature had recently swallowed ten boxes of quack pills.

I next visited a squalid cellar; and this time, taught by experience, I was at once sensible of the subtle vapours of the charcoal pot. A man, his wife - a miserable, broken-hearted looking woman - an old grand-dame, and two little children, were at their dinner. It consisted of coffee and bread. The place was underground. All the family slept in it, and all night long the charcoal pot glowed beside them. These people were Irish, and miserable creatures they were.

"Where's your daughter?" said my companion.

"Gone, gone," answered the mother. "She gets 6s. a week, and so she went plump over the door and left us."

"After all," said the poor father, "perhaps it's as well. When children grows up, their keep and their clothes take their wages fully."

The mother shook her head in obvious bitterness of spirit. They had a son who had served them in the same way.

"But surely," I said, "he comes to see you sometimes?"

"Niver, sir. He's ould enough to take care of himself, and he niver comes near us - niver."

In another cellar, or at least a sort of compromise between a groundfloor and a cellar, I found five combers at work. I congratulated them upon having a coal instead of a charcoal pot. The difference in the air was very striking, coming as I had done immediately out of the fumes of charcoal. The atmosphere here, although hot enough and impure enough, had a sweet genial taste - if I may use the word - compared with the charcoal-laden air. The latter felt at once hot, acrid, and bitter. The terms may be unphilosophical, but they convey an idea of the actual sensation.

In reply to my remark, the oldest man of the party said he could never stand the charcoal. It made him sick and giddy. But some masters had a prejudice in favour of it, and obliged their men to use it. Theirs was a poor trade. They had long, long hours, and they did not make more than 8s. or 9s. a week.

I asked whether the new machine affected them much? "It don't do us much good, any way," replied one.

"There's worse than the new machine for Englishmen," said another, "and that's the ship loads of them Irish that's coming among us, and pulling down the wage."

"There's no doubt of that," a third went on; "they don't live like Englishmen, them people."

"But if you dislike them so much," I said, "why do you teach them your trade?"

"We don't," said the first man. "No Englishman would, I hope."

"I'll tell you how it's done, sir," continued another. "There's old Irish hands here, and the new ones goes to them. Then the old ones gets a lot of work out from five or six masters, and gives it to the new ones to do, teaching them the way, and perhaps doing the job over if so be their scholars spoils the work; and so them persons, who are a sort of middle men like, pocket most of the wages that their countrymen earns."

"Aye," said the first comber, "and they don't sleep in beds, but on the wool."

"I heard tell," remarked the former speaker, "of a house were five-and-thirty on them pigged together on the floor."

Notwithstanding this display of animosity, my guide informed me that, on occasions of differences between the masters and the workmen, English and Irish pulled together in the most brotherly fashion.

During my investigations at Bradford I had more than one opportunity of seeing how the parochial authorities in agricultural districts pack their paupers off to the manufacturing regions. I select two cases. The first was that of a widow from a purely rural part of Yorkshire. She had a large young family. Her husband had been an agricultural labourer at 15s. a week in summer, and in winter he broke stones on the road for 15d. a day. On his death, the family became chargeable.

The parish immediately offered to pay the expense of removal, and gave the family £1 1s. if they would go to Bradford. They consented, and several of the children being sickly and subject to fits, so as to be unable to work in the mills, they have been mainly supported by Bradford ever since. The woman who told me these particulars said that she knew many families who had been sent to Bradford from the same locality in the same way.

The other case is that of a poor Irishwoman, one of the cleanest, tidiest, and the best specimens of her country people, in that walk of life, I have ever seen. Having heard of her case, she came out of the mill where she worked to speak to me, and conducted me to her chamber. A poorer one, and yet a cleaner one, I never saw; the deal table had been scoured until it shone again - there was a faded bit of carpeting on the floor, and not a speck of dust from wall to wall. I had never witnessed a more striking instance of cleanliness taking away all the squalor of poverty. In the room were three children. The eldest, a girl of seven, was rocking the cradle of the youngest, and attending to the proceedings of her other little sister.

"This is my housekeeper," said the mother, "and I can trust her and feel easy about the younger ones when I am at my work." The story of the family I shall relate nearly in the mother's words:

"My husband and me lived at Minstun (an agricultural district of Yorkshire). He was a handloom

51

weaver. Wages were very low, and times were very hard with us. We were at Minstun ten months, and in that time we tasted flesh twice. My poor husband had a consumption on him, and little by little he was forced to give up work. The farmers and the neighbours were very hard-hearted to us. They never sent as much as a ha'p'orth of milk even to the dying man.

When he was gone, the parish offered me and my four children 1s. to pay the rent each week, and 1s. to live on. If we didn't like that, they said, we might go to Bradford, and they would give us 30s. to move. They didn't give us 30s., but they gave us 29s., and we came here. If they had only given us 3s. a week I would have stayed.

I have a little boy, and I brought him to the mill, and told them all about us. The people at the mill were very kind, much kinder than the farmers. They took the little boy and set him to easy work, and gave him 2s. a week.

Then the manager said I might come into the mill and see him, and try if I couldn't learn to do something myself. So I got to know how to pick lumps out of the slubbings, and first I got 5s. 6d., and last week I was raised to 6s., so we have now 8s. a week.

Well, first I lived in a room belonging to the mill, with an outside stair, and I paid 1s. rent. But I was afraid of the children breaking their necks there. The only other place I could get near the mill was this. There are two rooms here, and the rent is 2s. I know it's too much for the like of me to pay, but think of the children. Well, sir, the parish are very good to me, and give me 3s. a week - 2s. for the rent and 1s. for coals - and we live and clothe ourselves on the other 8s.

We live chiefly on bread. I get a stone and a half of flour every week, and I bake it on Sundays. Then we have a little tea or coffee, and sometimes we have a little offal meat, because it's cheap. A good gentleman gave me the furniture I have and the bed in the other room. It cost altogether 15s.

Everybody has been kind to me, and the neighbours come in often to look after the children when I'm at work. I was born in Shandon parish, in Cork; and oh! I wish there were mills there for the poor to work in. It would be a blessing to them indeed."

LEEDS

LEEDS, as most people are aware, is the manufacturing capital of Yorkshire, as Manchester is of Lancashire. Each city is surrounded by a group of satellites, in some of which the enterprise and vigour of industry displayed excel even those of the district capitals. In the West, Stalybridge is popularly accounted a more " go-ahead " place than Manchester; and Blackburn takes the lead in point of speed of machinery. So, in the East, Huddersfield piques itself on producing finer broadcloths than Leeds; and Bradford boasts that it is absorbing the stuff manufacture of the larger town altogether to itself. Leeds, however, can very well afford to bear the prosperity of its young and growing rivals. It is, and will probably long continue to be, the real emporium of the cloth trade - while the preparation and spinning of flax is a branch of industry which belongs exclusively to itself.

A cluster of mud-huts stood where Leeds now stands as early as the signing of Magna Charta; and it was a considerable spinning and weaving place in the time of James I. His son granted municipal privileges to the town. The market days were then, as now, Tuesday and Saturday; and then, as now, the country manufacturers thronged in with their cloth, and exposed it for sale, not indeed in a porticoed hall, but on the parapet of the antique bridge which spanned the Aire. The Yorkshire, like the Lancashire mind, was grave, and somewhat Puritanic, in its instincts, and Cromwell invited Leeds to send a representative to the House of Commons. The Protectorate passed away, and Leeds thereafter continued unenfranchised until the Reform Bill.

In the reign of Charles II, the population of the district of Leeds is estimated, by Mr. Maculay, at 7,000. In 1801 the population of the township was 30,669. In 1831 it was 71,602. In 1841 it was 88,741, and it is now estimated as amounting to fully 100,000. The population of the parish of Leeds is 15,000. The value of life in Leeds - imperfect as its sanitary arrangements are, and grievously neglected as great and thickly-peopled ranges of its outskirts are left - is greater by a very considerable degree than in Manchester.

While upon this subject, it may not be amiss for me - as this is the last time I shall have the opportunity - to bring together the figures showing the rates of mortality in the principal cotton, woollen, and commercial towns in the North of England. In the cotton districts I take the representatives of all the types of cotton towns - the same in the woollen districts - and then I strike a mean between the value of male and female life, as given by the Registrar General's return:

COTTON TOWNS

In Blackburn there are living to one death	39	persons
" Bolton	37	"
" Ashton and Oldham	37	"
" Preston .... ,.........................	38	"
" Manchester	30	"

Showing the mean number of deaths in the cotton towns to be one for every 36 1-5th of the population.

55

WOOLLEN AND WORSTED TOWNS

In Huddersfield there are living to one death   50 persons
" Dewsbury ....   47 "
" Halifax ....   47 "
" Bradford ....   40 "
" Leeds ....   38 "

Showing the mean number of deaths in the woollen and worsted towns to be one for every 44 2-5th of the population.

Taking the two great shipping ports of the two counties, we find that the proportions of deaths is reversed. In Liverpool, one person dies out of every 29. In Hull, one person out of every 35. Still, the latter place seems the worst, in a sanitary view, in Yorkshire. In Sheffield one person dies to every 36½ of the population. So that Leeds stands, in its own county, the third from the bottom of the list.

By the census of 1841, there appear to have been in Leeds 34,002 inhabited and 2,419 uninhabited buildings. The latter at present include about 15 churches of the Establishment, containing sitting room for about 20,000 persons - and upwards of 30 dissenting places of worship, affording seating room for about 30,000.

Of these latter the Wesleyans possess six chapels, the New Connexion Methodists 3, the Association Methodists 2, the Primitive Methodists 2, the Teetotal Methodists 1, the Independents 5, the Particular Baptists 1, the General Baptists 1, the Society of Friends 1, the Presbyterians 1, and the Unitarians, Swedenborgians, and Inghamites 1 each. A new Established Church is at present being built by the Messrs. Marshall. Most of the places of worship named above have, as in Lancashire, Sunday schools attached to them. The number of scholars is estimated at about 12,000.

In Leeds, as in Manchester, a great proportion of poor-law relief is out-door. At present trade is brisk, and but for the recent visitation of cholera, which threw a great number of widows and orphans upon the parish, the pressure upon the rates would be light. As it is, the amount of out-door relief weekly administered is about £350.

Leeds has little or none of that hothouse appearance which to some extent distinguishes Manchester. It seems, in its physical peculiarities, a more substantial and slower-growing town than its high-pressure cotton neighbour, and it possesses none of the metropolitan attributes of the latter.

Leeds has no public parks. With here and there an exceptional spot, the suburbs extend, in mean, clumsy, straggling streets, out into the bare country. There are no such fair ranges of villas as those which, in many quarters, skirt the busy portions of Manchester; and the dwellings of the labouring class, to which I shall speedily call particular attention, are, in point of appearance - and of symmetrical outward and convenient inward arrangement - decidedly inferior to those of the cotton capital.

A locality on which I cannot but bestow a few descriptive words is the Cloth Hall - or, rather, the Cloth Halls - for there are two for different kinds of stuff in Leeds. The manufacture of cloth has always been to a greater or less extent domestic. Out of the vast quantity of yarn or thread manufactured from the flax in Leeds, very little is converted into cloth in the town.

The weavers live scattered in the neighbouring villages, working for different masters, who, on Tuesdays and Saturdays, by themselves or their agents, expose the goods for sale in the Cloth Hall. The business is carried on with that curious taciturn regularity, amounting to a sort of industrial discipline, which specially characterises the buyers and sellers of the North.

The Hall which I visited is a plain brick building forming a quadrangle, in which the grass grows, and which was crowded with carts ready to take away the goods. The building consists simply of four long corridors forming a square. Two narrow tables run the whole length of each corridor. A stance about three feet long is apportioned to each manufacturer, and his name and residence are inscribed upon the table between the painted boundaries which divide him from his neighbours.

The hour arrives, a bell rings, the doors are flung open to purchasers, and there, ranged all down the long bazaar - or "streets" as they are called - stands each vendor, silent and erect behind the counter, with his goods heaped up before him. There is a sort of Oriental taciturnity and reserve in the whole aspect of the affair. No man solicits custom. No man wishes to be informed what he can tempt the buyer with next. The merchant walks slowly down the "street". If his eye fall upon a parcel of goods, the vendor silently unfolds the cloth to show its gloss and texture. If the lot does not suit, not a word is spoken; if it does, the price is merely named, and the transaction is concluded in an instant.

Five minutes before the close of an hour the bell rings again. The clock strikes in due time, and the market is ended. A fine is imposed upon any manufacturer who lingers even five minutes after the stipulated time is up. Of those connected with the woollen trade only cloth merchants are admitted into the market; no stapler, for instance, is allowed to be present for a moment.

So much for the sale of cloth. I have already described its manufacture in my letter upon Huddersfield and Dewsbury. It will, perhaps be for the advantage of the reader, before I touch upon the sanitary and social condition of the population of Leeds, that I describe the process of manufacture of what I may call the second staple of the place - the dressing of flax, and the spinning therefrom of linen and tow yarns and threads.

There are about a dozen flax establishments in Leeds, the largest of which is the celebrated mill of the Messrs. Marshall - a concern employing from 1,200 to 1,500 hands, and paying about £600 a week in wages.[1]

As in the worsted trade, the vast majority of the hands employed in the flax mills are women and children; but, unlike the worsted trade, there is no such branch of industry as wool-combing to employ the male adults. In Leeds, a considerable proportion of the husbands and brothers of the female flax-workers find employment in the cloth trade; but it is not easy to ascertain how the numbers of boys employed in some of the mills - that of the Messrs. Marshall for example - are provided for after they have outgrown their labour in

---

[1] For an account of the firm, see W. G. Rimmer. *Marshall's of Leeds, Flax Spinners. 1700-1886*, Cambridge, 1960.

the heckling of flax and the carding of tow. As in the case, however, of all manufacturing processes, they are needed and they appear. They perform their spell of duty, and are then absorbed into other occupations.

Of course, the work being so managed, the average of wages paid in flax-mills is a low one. As in the case of worsted, but unlike the cases of wool and cotton, the weavers gain the highest pay; but the quantity of linen woven in the Leeds flax-mills is very small. The threads are often exported. and of those woven in this country, Barnsley, in Yorkshire, takes and works up into fabric the greatest quantity.

The flax manufacture, in all its stages save one, is a cleanly and healthful occupation. The objectionable process is the necessary one of heckling - analogous, so far as the difference in the staple material will permit of comparison, to the willowing of wool and the cleaning and blowing of cotton. The dust produced in the heckling process is very considerable, and it is a dust of a more injurious character - hard, subtle, fine and penetrating. Even in the best ventilated and most carefully regulated mills, it flies in clouds, which dim the extremities of the room; and I have experienced an effect from it, which not even shoddy dust produced - a smarting and a watering of the eyes. The heads and shoulders of the work people are plentifully strewn with this sharp dry powder; and although in well-ordered mills the machines etc. are cleaned thrice a day, an hour's work is sufficient to coat them again with a dun layer of dust and filament.

In coarse spinning establishments, and in the process of evolving the large loose yarn made from tow, there is another unpleasantness of a minor nature. Flaxen threads are always conducted in the spinning process through hot water - and when the threads are large, loose, and spongy, the whirling motion of the spindles on which they are wound flings the moisture about in all directions. Splashboards of different constructions are in use, and in some establishments the tenters wear thick leather aprons; but the result is always to make the place sloppy, and the air, particularly in winter, disagreeably and unhealthily damp.

These drawbacks excepted - and the second is very partial in occurrence as well as minor in nature - flax dressing and spinning may be counted as amongst the healthiest and cleanliest of factory processes.

The sorters first operate upon the flax. They are male adults, and their labour is skilled. They therefore earn the fair wage of from £1 1s. to £1 5s. The boys who assist them, and who are learning, are paid about 5s. The next process is "breaking". The boy who tends the necessary machine feeds it with the raw material, which, passing between the crushing wheels, emerges bruised and pliable from the tremendous pressure. One boy is sufficient to look after each machine, under the eye of a superintendent. The former earns about 4s. 6d.; the superintendents, I may add, throughout the different operations, are paid from 20s, to 25s. weekly.

The heckling comes next. Here great numbers of children are employed. They screw the bunches of flax tight to iron rods, which, being placed in the centre of a complicated and powerful piece of machinery, the flax is subjected to the shining steel teeth or heckles, which, set in a circular frame-work, revolve rapidly, and rend and comb the substance just as the float-boards of a paddle-wheel strike the water. The refuse flax thus torn away is tow; the remainder, combed into soft smooth locks, is called "line", and ultimately forms the thread of linen. This is the dusty and unhealthy process which I mentioned. It is usually conducted almost altogether by children, girls and boys.

In the heckling room in Messrs. Marshall's mill about 130 children are employed. Some of the girls there wore handkerchiefs over their mouths in the manner of the shoddy grinders. A number of "half-timers" - children from eight to thirteen years of age - work at this process in the mill in question.

I was struck by their appearance, not only as presenting the greatest number of young children labouring in a body which I have yet seen, but as exhibiting a greater amount of labour performed - of continuous active exertion going on - than I have yet found requisite in any branch of any manufacturing process. There is hardly a moment of inactivity. The flax has to be taken up in locks, screwed into its frame, placed on the heckling machine, taken off, and the supply constantly renewed. When I say that the young children - toiling so quickly and dexterously, amid the flying dust and the whirling mechanism, every limb and every finger in rapid and continuous play - had a strange elfish appearance, which I have never before remarked in any department of juvenile industry. I only use the expression to convey an idea which struck me forcibly as I beheld the scene of labour.

The wages paid to these young labourers are small enough in all conscience. The half-timers do not earn above from 1s. 6d. to 1s. 8d. a week. The elder children make double the amount. They are, of course, superintended by overlookers.

The first of a long series of "drawing" operations comes next, identical in principle with the drawing processes which I have so often had occasion to describe. The flax is drawn into what I may call a set of ribbons, each narrower and thinner but more compact than the preceding, until it becomes a mere strip of exquisite fineness, when it is loosely twisted upon large bobbins - having thus arrived at the state of yarn. All these drawing processes are superintended exclusively by girls and women - one to each frame.

The work is very light. Indeed, so far as any muscular exertion goes, the tenters are really idle half their time. I have seen the majority of them seated and quietly watching their frames, without at all neglecting their duty. It is only, indeed, any accidental flaw in the material, or irregularity in the mechanism, which calls them into action. The wages of these girls are from 5s. to 5s. 6d. per week.

The yarn has now to be spun. The operation is performed, as in the case of worsted, upon frames. The atmosphere of the spinning-room is kept warm by the quantity of hot water through which the threads are passed; but the temperature is not so high as in fine-spinning cotton factories. It may range from 76° to 80°. The spinners, like the drawers, are all women and girls. A young person of from fifteen to eighteen years of age is preferred, as having the finest touch for the repair of broken threads. The wages of the spinners are sometimes high, but not always, a shade higher than those of the drawing-frame tenters.

The reelers, who work by the piece, and whose duty it is to reel the threads off the bobbins into skeins and hanks, form the next set of workpeople. They are generally grown-up women, and the most expert and industrious amongst them can make about 8s. a week. The simple reeling frame being driven round by hand, the labour of its attendants is not regulated by the motion of the steam-engine, and they frequently continue their toil while the rest of the hands are at dinner. The winders are, however, obliged in beginning and leaving off work, to conform to factory hours.

I have said that comparatively little linen cloth is prepared in Leeds, and that still less is woven by power in the mills. In the Messrs. Marshall's establishment the small amount of weaving performed is entirely carried on by women, their wages being stated to me as ranging from 8s. to 9s. per week.

The reader will recollect that in the heckling process the tow is separated from the "line". The former is then carried to another department, where it is carded, drawn, and spun into coarser threads. The wages earned by the workpeople are almost the same as those paid in the finer department of the trade. The dust in the tow carding room is very considerable, and the floating filament abundant and annoying. No allowance whatever is made to the hands employed in the heckling and tow-carding rooms in consideration of the unpleasant and unwholesome nature of their occupation. Indeed, I cannot find, in the whole range of textile manufacturing industry, that an advanced rate of wages is given for any unhealthy occupation, nominally or really, on account of its injuriousness.

In all the flax-mills which I have seen, provisions, more or less ample, are made for ventilation. Where swinging panes are adopted, however, the workpeople are too often apt to shut them. In Mr. Morfitt's flax mill I found that the hands in the spinning room had voluntarily deprived themselves of fresh air because the day was boisterous and rainy. Mr. Marshall's establishment is scientifically ventilated - a fanner, driven by an eight-horse power engine, being employed to fan the air up through gratings in the floor into the large room.

This large room is one of the sight of Leeds, and a sight amply worth seeing. Having some short time ago had occasion to add very largely to their original establishment, the Messrs. Marshall conceived the idea of constructing a mill in which all the processes of flax manufacture, save those of sorting and heckling, should be conducted on one level and in one vast hall This design they carried out. The hall occupies two acres, the roof is supported by 66 iron pillars, and the whole is lighted by 66 glass cupolas. The coup d'oeil of this vast apartment, crowded from wall to wall with busy machinery, tented by hundreds of active and healthy-looking young women, is a very fine as well as a curious and interesting spectacle. The atmosphere, except in the spinning portion of the room, is perfectly cool and pleasant. The cleanliness preserved is perfect. The girls, I was informed, take a pride in scouring and keeping bright the portion of stone floor over which each presides. The frames are provided with boxes, where the girls keep those articles of dress which they lay aside for working costume when in the mill.

The dinner hour arrived when I was in the room, and there was a general production and application of clothes and shoe-brushes preparatory to leaving the establishment. The roof of this vast room is as curious in its way as the interior. It is perfectly flat, and covered with grass - the cupolas rising from the green expanse like so many fairy tents of crystal.

THE ROOF OF MARSHALL'S ONE-STORIED FLAX MILL.

Among the few weaving establishments in Leeds is an old riding school, which has been converted into a loom shop, and gives occupation to nearly 100 weavers and winders. The place is of course merely a shell crowded with hand-looms.

The stuff woven is woollen, with occasionally a mixture of cotton. The weavers are men, women, boys and girls. Some of the latter wind for their grown-up relatives. These weavers work for a large firm, and have pretty constant work. Their average wages may be about 10s. or 10s. 6d. a week. About 1d. in the shilling is paid to the winder, and the rent for each loom is 3d. per week.

The hours of labour are regular and long - from six a.m. until half-past eight p.m., allowing half-an-hour for breakfast, an hour for dinner, and half-an-hour for tea. In summer the hours are from five a.m. until eight p.m.

When whole families work in the establishment, the superintendent tries to group each of them together. Parents will bring their children, and pay for a loom for them to learn at, and when they can do a little coarse work they begin to receive a small salary.

As I stood between two looms, the foreman told me that the job on the one would bring in about 8s. 6d. and the other about 12s. a week. The best webs were given out as impartially as possible. Their house employed many domestic weavers, but when work was slack those under the immediate control and inspection of the firm had the preference.

"Since bread and food have been so cheap," continued the foreman, "almost all of us who are industrious may have a bit of meat for dinner every day. But when provisions were twice as high, when flour was 4s. a stone, we had no better wages than now, and not half so much work. I have seen this room half empty - half the looms standing - because the prices of everything to eat were so high that people had no money to buy aught else; but now everyone of us has as much work as he can put his face to."

This man, an exceedingly intelligent person, went on to condemn the common Yorkshire system of providing only two rooms in a working man's house, as being neither decent nor wholesome.

"It might do," he said, "for the Irish, who would always live together by families to save house rent, but it ought not to be tolerated by Englishmen."

From something which I heard in this establishment, I proceeded to the neighbouring row of cottages recently erected. These had each a common room, a bedroom, and a cellar loom-shop. In the first which I entered two Irishmen were weaving a coarse sacking, and the wife of one of them was winding in the bare, scarcely-furnished room on the ground floor. The tenant of the house told me that the row was all alike, and belonged to the gentleman for whom he was working. The two looms were fixtures; of course, therefore, he could not rent them without renting the house. The rent was stopped every week out of his wages. Whatever they were, much or little, the rent must always come out of them before he got the money. He believed the work was given to him just to enable him to pay the rent (which was 3s. weekly), and thus to make a good return for the money invested in the houses; otherwise, it would be cheaper for the master to get the stuff woven by power. His wages, with his wife to wind, were very small, not averaging above 9s. or 10s. at the highest.

From another source I learnt that many of the poor weavers inhabiting houses built upon a similar plan, and with a similar view, had suffered most severely during the last season of depression. It often happened that their wages were entirely absorbed by their rent, while the parish refused them assistance on the very reasonable plea, that a man who was paying 3s. of weekly rent could not be said to be an object of charity. Thus these poor people had no means of obtaining work, except from a quarter which would give it them only on condition that they paid back all or the greater part of their remuneration in rent.

In good times, of course, a weaver need not be so hard driven; but if a master, having work for ten men, and being also the landlord of ten houses, says to twenty men seeking employment, "I shall give my work to the ten who will consent to live in my ten houses, and pay me a high rent for them," then assuredly the scheme, if it does not actually amount to the truck system, is a very close imitation of it.

I admit, with pleasure, that the houses were decided improvements on the general run of labourers' dwellings in Leeds. Indeed another row which I visited - newly built, and devoted to cloth hand-loom weaving - were most excellently arranged; roomy, airy, and in every respect comfortable; but, with regard to them, the same, or, at all events, a similar system was in operation.

The house in the row in question in which I found the most intelligent tenant was fitted up somewhat like the silk-weavers' cottages at Macclesfield. The loom-shop was on the attic floor; the looms in operation were four, of which three were fixtures belonging to the house; and the tenant had of course the preference when work was slack over those weavers who wrought for the landlord, but who did not live in any of his houses or work by his loom.

I have said that the house was most excellent; it contained a half cellar, or rather area, sitting room, a kitchen, with sink and water laid on, a ground-floor parlour, and two bedrooms. The rent was 5s. 6½d. per week, and it must be paid the first thing out of the weekly earnings.

In answer to my question, the weaver said that the distinct understanding was that, if by any chance, in any week, he only earned 5s. 6½d. then the whole of his earnings during that week must go to pay the rent.

His family worked for him. If he had no family he would let out the looms, which were constructed for weaving broadcloth, at Is. each. For the best jobs he could earn from 13s. to 14s.; the inferior sorts of work produced about 10s.

In his house they laboured from six a.m. until seven p.m.; and they very often did not take more than a quarter of an hour to dinner. They mostly had a bit of meat for dinner every day, but many had to make tea and coffee and bread serve them.

"Sir," concluded the weaver, "don't you think that a skilled, hard-working, sober man, with a family to feed, ought to be able to earn a pound a week, if everything was as it should be? There's few Englishmen would grudge hard labour if they felt that they were so paid for it that they could live wholesomely and bring up their families in decency and independence."

This house-trucking system is not confined in Leeds altogether to cottages fitted up with looms, and of which the loom is in reality a part. In connection with at least one mill, I shall not specify its nature, a similar system prevails. The proprietor has built a number of cottages for his labourers, and these cottages must be occupied. Of course all the mill hands do not live on their master's property, because the number of cottages is comparatively inconsiderable - but not a hand will get employment in the factory should he refuse to occupy any of them which may become vacant.

I think I mentioned a somewhat similar case in Bolton, when to each mule a house-key was attached, which the spinner was bound to pay rent for.

Now in many instances I have had to praise the style of cottage erected by the millowner for his people, and to praise, also, the spirit in which the undertaking seemed to be conducted. Masters and men have assured me that the renting, on the part of the working people, of these cottages was perfectly voluntary. There the houses stood ready. They were superior to the ordinary run of operative dwellings; they were conveniently near to the mill, and they were cheap. As a natural consequence they never wanted occupants.

If, however, on the other hand, the holding of a cottage be made in any case compulsory upon any mill-hand, the result is simply that he is obliged to take out a part of his wages in goods - these goods in the present instance consisting of house-room. This is a matter to which public attention may well be directed.

In all the cases which I have specified the master holds in his own hand the fund from which his rent is paid; and in hard times, let others suffer as they may, he - at all events so long as any wages at all are paid - is certain of the interest and profit on his own building speculation.

As to the truck system in general, from all the inquiries which I can make, I learn that virtually it is abolished. Railway excavators were perhaps the last class which, as a class, suffered from it. Here and there, no doubt, relics of the practice still linger - the parties being small manufacturers, often located in out-of-the-way country places, where the occasional difficulty of obtaining commodities gives some semblance of excuse for the practice. But even in these instances the offence is so disguised, there are so many links of agency employed, and so many quirks and quibbles resorted to, that the difficulty of making out a legal case is almost insuperable.

Instances have occurred in the Bradford district, but the authorities have in vain endeavoured to prove legally what no one doubted morally. For all practical purposes, however, the "Tommy-shop" may be considered as finally shut up in the manufacturing districts.

There are two classes of operatives' houses in Leeds, and the first and worst species includes fully three-fourths of the workmen's tenements in the borough. These are the two-roomed dwellings known as the "House and Chamber" class of abodes. In nine cases out of ten they are inferior to the cotton workers' houses in furniture, cleanliness, and neatness. I have been in the dwellings of many of the flax hands, and found them not only poor and uncomfortable, but in frequent instances squalid.

The clothworkers, having higher wages, are very generally better off; and the quarter which they principally inhabit - the west part of the town - is, of the operative districts, decidedly the best, in point of building, paving, draining and cleansing. Still even their dwellings are not what they ought to be; and altogether I am compelled, after a minute and searching survey of the town, to say that the domestic condition of the working population of Leeds seems to me lower than that of any manufacturing town which I have yet investigated.

Between Leeds and Huddersfield the difference in favour of the latter is palpable and distinct, and yet a great portion of the work people of both towns labour in the same branches of trade, and receive the same, or nearly the same, amount of remuneration.

The very low wages paid in the flax trade, the consequence of girls and children being chiefly - indeed, for all practical purposes, exclusively - employed, seems to me to tend strongly towards dragging down the standard of living and of domestic comfort, even of the better paid artizans.

At all events, be the cause what it may, the clothworkers of Leeds, although they live in better dwellings, and in greater comfort than the flax workers of that town, do not live in such good dwellings, or in such great comfort, as the clothworkers of Huddersfield. In all my peregrinations in the manufacturing capital of Yorkshire, I have not discovered a single operative dwelling with a back and front entrance, and consequently a through current of air.

One man, indeed, said that he thought double houses were more wholesome than single ones, because they were snugger and warmer.

"One heats the other," he said; "like sleeping two in a bed."

The illustration sums up the arguments against the practice. In a large proportion of the houses in question, the family, except when all are grown up, sleep together in the higher room. Beds in the lower rooms are, however, not uncommon. The furniture seldom shows the commonly existing neat comfort, or the less frequently occurring pretension, which mark Manchester tenements of different grades. A parlour-kitchen can be made, after its own fashion, a very cheerful apartment. Many a one have I recently visited, in which the gleam of a good fire was playing on polished pot-lids, and glancing crockery, arranged tidily and orderly upon the well-scoured racks, the floor either carpeted with a decent drugget, or nicely and brightly sanded - many a house of this class, I repeat, I have lately entered, in which the sensation of comfort was very decidedly in the ascendant. But in Leeds, I have found, as a general rule, domestic utensils coarser and scantier, and the spirit of neatness and good housewifery manifested on rarer occasions and in a slighter degree.

The second and better class of houses, which form the minority, possess a sunken parlour-kitchen, half the window of which only rises above the pavement. Above this apartment are placed two rooms in the ordinary manner. The sunken story is not quite a cellar, and in many instances I found it dry, warm, and cheerful. When it exists the groundfloor room is very generally half unfurnished, the family making the lower apartment their ordinary living place. Good cooking-ranges are abundant. Water is seldom introduced into the houses; the stand-tap system being the usual one, each cock serving a greater or a smaller number of houses, according to the comparative poverty of the locality.

The rents range, for the medium class of dwellings, from 1s. 6d. to 3s. weekly. The houses letting for the former sum are often rickety old places, in bad repair, and with small close rooms. In almost every case the house-door is the parlour-door. Even in the very superior house rented at 5s. 6½d. by the cloth weaver, a visit to which I have above described, there was no lobby, the door only separating the best room in the house from the street.

An institution in Leeds has recently been opened in connection with the workhouse, a visit to which gave me very high gratification. It is the industrial school for pauper children; and an establishment more perfect in its architectural arrangements, and so far as I could judge, in its system of discipline and training, I never saw.[1] The industrial school, a handsome Elizabethan structure, stands in the midst of six acres of land belonging to it, on the brow of a declivity, removed by about half a mile from the smoke and foulness of the town. It has now been open rather more than a year. The average number of pupils may be stated at 150, and as yet only two deaths have occurred in the establishment. During the prevalence of cholera in Leeds, not even a case of diarrhoea occurred in the industrial school, and when I visited it, although I found a few children in the infirmary, none were so ill as to be in bed. A circumstance, however, indicating a sanitary feature of the district, is that the institution possesses two rooms with particularly constructed blinds, for cases of sore eyes. Although neither of these apartments were darkened on my visit, three or four of the children in the infirmary wore green shades. Mr. Hisk, the master of the establishment, thinks that these cases are very frequently of scrofulous origin.

---

[1] The Leeds Industrial School, Beckett Street, in the same grounds as the workhouse. In 1906 part of it was incorporated in the extension to what is now St. James's Hospital.

Nothing can exceed the exquisite neatness and cleanliness which pervade the establishment, to its most insignificant corner. The children themselves, under the superintendence of paid servants - for very properly no adult pauper is suffered to come within the walls - perform the household duties. The object is to bring up the pupils for domestic servants and apprentices.

The girls learn to cook, scour, wash, iron, sew, and make their own dresses. The boys do the rougher cleaning work, and, under the superintendence of a gardener, raise the greater part of the vegetables consumed in the institution. The trades taught the boys are shoemaking and tailoring, so that the school will speedily be, so far, self-supplying. All the boys are exercised in spade husbandry.

Of course it is the elder boys who are taught mechanical trades. The younger ones go to school every day, and the tailors, shoemakers, washers, ironers, etc., have three days' school and three days' work. I visited the tailoring, shoemaking, and sewing-room. In the first the average number of boys who had worked during the previous week was seven. The amount of work done was twenty articles, such as jackets, trousers, and waistcoats repaired, three new jackets made, and one waistcoat.

In the shoemaking room, the average number of workers had been six. They had repaired eighteen pairs of boys' and girls' shoes, made five new pairs, and an odd one. Two pairs were in progress.

In the sewing-room, the number of girls employed had been six or eight. They had made ten shirts, and mended fifteen. They had mended twenty-six chemises and ten bed-gowns; mended thirty-four pinafores and made a dozen; bound seven pairs of shoes, run seven pairs of stockings, and darned about 145 pairs.

About a dozen boys have been already apprenticed, and a dozen girls sent out to service. They are doing well, and applications for the children come in faster than the establishment is as yet able to supply them. Certainly there will seem to be less durability in early impressions than is generally believed, if the boys and girls brought up, in the Leeds Industrial School fall into habits of slovenliness and sloth.

The dietary adopted is, in its essential parts, that of the workhouse, consisting of meat thrice a week, and soups and puddings on the off days; but in all essential features care is wisely taken to place no obvious pauper stamp upon the institution, and to banish as much as may be, the workhouse associations from the children's minds.

A popular co-operative institution in Leeds, similar to none which I have seen, is working in a building called the "People's Mill", close to the Messrs. Marshall's factory.[1] The "People's Mill" grinds corn of all kinds, and supplies to its large circle of proprietors flour and grain, perfectly unadulterated, and as near cost price as the actual working expenses will permit. The number of members is about 3,000, and the vast majority are working men. Each pays £1 1s. entrance money. There is no yearly subscription.

---

[1] The "People's Mill" began operations in 1847 in Saville Street, but removed to Marshall Street. Holbeck, at the beginning of 1849. The Leeds Flour Society, later the Leeds District Flour Mill 'Society, was the forerunner of the Leeds Industrial Co-operative Society.

The average amount annually saved to the subscribers was computed by the managing miller, whom I found upon the premises, as about equal to each member's subscription - that is to say, the flour in the mill can be had so much cheaper than the same flour in the shops as to save an ordinary family about a pound in the year.

The great advantage, however, looked to is the purity of the article. No member is allowed to hold more than one share, or to receive more flour than is necessary for the consumption of his own family; and any member selling bread of the society's flour is, for a second offence, expelled. The only similar institution in Yorkshire is at Hull.

The cotton-town practice of dosing children with narcotics does not prevail to any great extent in the woollen or worsted districts. Still it does more or less exist. The relieving officer at Bradford told me that he had broken many a bottle of Godfrey; and in Leeds paregoric is not infrequently sold by the small general dealers.

Narcotic drugs are more or less taken by adults in all manufacturing towns, and in Leeds opium chewers (often women) are not unfrequent. A medical gentleman in large practice among the poor informed me that, in times of manufacturing distress, he has seen people reduced to a state bordering on *delirium tremens* for want of means to purchase the usual laudanum dram.

The same gentleman added that Ophthalmia was not unfrequently produced by the excessively penetrating and irritating nature of the dust in flax-heckling and tow-carding rooms. The substance in question also produced a throat complaint similar to "shoddy fever". There is indeed a shoddy trade in the flax districts as well as in the cloth. Old ropes are untwisted as old rags are unpicked, and the unravelled hemp is heckled and wrought up again into a coarser sort of sacking. The dust produced by the old hemp heckling is, as may be well conceived, stifling.

The corporation of Leeds is, I understand, about to spend a very large sum, about £30,000 or £40,000, in the formation of an extensive system of paving, drainage, etc., in hitherto neglected portions of the borough. Never were sanitary reforms more imperatively called for. The condition of vast districts of the opulent and important town of Leeds is such as the very strongest language cannot over-state.

Virulent and fatal as was the recent attack of cholera here, my wonder is that cholera, or some disease almost equally fatal, is ever absent. From one house, for instance, situated in a large irregular court or yard - a small house containing two rooms - four corpses were recently carried. I looked about and did not marvel. The whole vicinage was two or three inches deep in filth. This seemed to be the normal state even of the passable parts of the place. In the centre of the open space was a cluster of pigsties, privies, and cesspools - bursting with pent-up abominations; and half a dozen paces from this delectable nucleus was a pit, about five-feet square, filled to the very brim with semi-liquid manure gathered from stables and houses around. This yard lies on the south side of the Aire, not more than a gunshot from Leeds Bridge .

The east and north-east districts of Leeds are, perhaps, the worst. A short walk from the Briggate, in the direction in which Deansgate branches off from the main entry, will conduct the visitor into a perfect wilderness of foulness. Conceive an acre of little streets, run up without attention to plan or health - acre on acre of closely-built and thickly-peopled ground, without a paving-stone upon the surface, or an inch of sewer beneath, deep trodden-churned slough of mud forming the only thoroughfares - here and there an open space, used not exactly as the common cess-pool, but as the common cess-yard of the vicinity - in its centre, ash-pits employed for dirtier purposes than containing ashes - privies often ruinous, almost horribly foul - pig-stys very commonly left *pro tempore* untenanted, because their usual inmates have been turned out to prey upon the garbage of the neighbourhood.

Conceive streets, and courts, and yards which a scavenger never appears to have entered since King John incorporated Leeds, and which in fact give the idea of a town built in a slimy bog.

Conceive such a surface drenched with the liquid slops which each family flings out daily and nightly before their own threshold, and further fouled by the malpractices of children, for which the parents and not the children deserve shame and punishment.

Conceive, in short, a whole district to which the above description rigidly and truthfully applies, and you will, I am sorry to say, have a fair idea of what at present constitutes a large proportion of the operative part of Leeds. I have seen here and there in Bradford spots very nearly, and in Halifax spots quite as bad; but here it is no spot - the foulness over large sections of the town, particularly towards the suburbs, constitutes the very face and essence of things. I have plodded by the half hour through streets in which the undisturbed mud lay in wreaths from wall to wall, and across open spaces, overlooked by houses all around, in which the pigs, wandering from this central oasis, seemed to be roaming through what was only a large sty. Indeed, pigs seem to be the natural inhabitants of such places. I think they are more common in some parts of Leeds than dogs and cats are in others; and wherever they abound, wherever the population is filthiest, there are the houses the smallest, the rooms the closest, and the most overcrowded.

One characteristic of such localities is a curious and significant one. Before almost every house-door there lies, of course, until the pig comes upon the deposit, a little heap of boiled-out tea leaves. Although all the domestic refuse is flung out, you hardly ever see bones, but the tea-pot is evidently in operation at every meal. Here and there, I ought to add, the visitor will, even in the midst of such scenes as I have tried to sketch, come upon a cluster or a row of houses better than ordinary, and through the almost invariably open doors of which he will see some indications of domestic comfort; but such buildings are the exceptions - and, exceptions as they are, they rise out of the same slough of mud and filth, and command the same ugly sights as their neighbours.

There is, I believe, a Nuisance Committee in Leeds. I inquired whether they were aware of even the most flagrant of all these sanitary enormities. Had their attention, for instance, been ever drawn to the practice of keeping pigs, or rather letting the pigs keep themselves, in crowded neighbourhoods?

"Yes," I was answered, by a gentleman much interested in the subject, "Yes, I have reported these things over and over again, until I was sick and tired of reporting; but, you see, nothing has been done."

Referring to the opening sentence of this communication it is to be hoped that Leeds is on the eve of a sanitary revolution, and that what is true of the town today will be but historic a twelve-month hence. Things are at present so palpably bad, that even a small outlay would make an immense change for the better. Even if it be impracticable to construct at once a thorough system of house sewerage, or to lay down at once miles of substantial paving, it would be surely easy, by means of the police, to compel the observance of something like ordinary human decency in the habits of children, to clean out and render available revolting cesspools, and to make a devastating razzia amongst those foul nuisances - in a crowded and often a fever-smitten locality - the pigs and pig-sties.

In one respect Leeds is superior to most of its great industrial neighbours. Owing to its more easterly position it is not so exposed to descents of vast masses of Irish poverty as are the towns of Lancashire; and owing to the second staple of the place being flax, a certain proportion of the Irish who do not reach Leeds have been more or less trained to industrious habits, amid the wreck of their linen manufacture in their own country.

In Leeds I have, for the first time, found considerable numbers of Irishmen steadily working at the loom. Most of them had learned the work at home, and had followed the track when it left their shores. They had all the same story to tell, of work scanty and wages low, compared with what they had been in Dublin. I found many of these weavers employed upon the coarsest sort of stuff, such as sacking and canvas. One of them said that forty of his countrymen whom he knew were working in Leeds, and that they sent their children to the flax mills. The Irish, however, he added, who came from parts of the country which had never been manufacturing, kept their children very often at home, and bred them up to any sort of little trade which they themselves followed. This is a species of education which I suspect is very often equivalent to breeding up the children with no trade at all.

In one house, for instance, I found an old Irishman, in the receipt of parish relief, with his grand-daughter, a stout girl of 13 at the very least, seated by the fire.

"The poor thing," said the old man, "wasn't fit to go to one of them mills. Why, sure they would, may be, maim her. Childer was maimed there every day."

I asked whether she went to school.

"Not at present," was the reply; "but she has been ever since she was three years of age, till lately."

I was rather surprised to hear, as a pendant to this statement, that the scholar did not know her letters.

Three of the ordinary trades of the Irish in Leeds are rag-picking - such as I have described it in Batley, near Dewsbury - untwisting old ropes, and mat-making. Men and women generally work at the latter employment; but the women almost invariably hawk the produce about for sale. I visited two cellars in one of the Irish streets, in each of which I found a man and woman preparing mats. A sentence of description will suffice for both apartments. They might be about seven feet square, littered with old bagging, Russia mats, old ropes, and shavings - furnished with rickety deal tables, and two or three chairs more or less dilapidated, and a bed, in one case, spread on a low frame, in the other, rolled up in a corner. The cooking apparatus, in both cases, consisted of a single pot. Miserable as these abodes are, they were clearly superior to the Irish cellars in Manchester and Oldham.

The people in the second cellar were rather better off than those in the first, because the wife had a "good connection" in the matselling business, and could more generally realise fair prices for her wares. In both instances the people gave me every information about their trade; and I subjoin the substance of their statements, which in the main agreed.

"We make two sorts of mats - rope mats which are the best sort, and stitched mats. Both of these mats are principally made of a stuff called `dewit'."

This dewit was a substance like long clusters of coarse hemp.

"We buy it for 3s. a stone. We then dye it brown with catechu; we dye it by boiling a stone of it, with 1½d. worth of catechu, and then we rinse it out with clean water and a little alum, and hang it up to dry."

The side of each room was clothed with clusters of the stuff in question.

"We have next to get ropes for the rope mats, and old sacking and shavings and twine for the stitched mats. The ropes cost about 1s. 3d. per stone. The old bagging comes to about 1¼d. per mat, and the twine and Russia matting a trifle more. We use shavings when we can get them for nothing. To make a good-sized rope mat, like what we sell for a gentleman's door, takes six or seven pounds of rope, and from a pound to a pound and a half of dewit. We generally count, working up the waste of one with another, that 16 lbs. of dewit will make three rope mats. Stitched mats do not take more than half that quantity, but they require, besides the sacking, twine and garden mats."

The rope mats are made upon the principle of weaving. The strands of untwisted ropes are stretched across a frame, exactly like warps, and then the workman, passing a stronger rope in the manner of a woof across them, binds into the twisted cord-locks of the dewit, which forms the superficies of the mat. In the stitched sort the dewit is fastened by coarse needlework - to the sacking. One of the mat workers I saw was an old man. He could, he said, once have made four or five rope mats a day. Now he could not make more in a week. The stitched sort required a day to make two, and another day was generally requisite to sell them.

The woman in the first cellar stated, in regard to the sale, as follows: "I sell the mats we make here, and it's very hard work - much harder than making them, and very uncertain. The prices I get depend mostly altogether upon whether it's poor houses or rich houses I sell at. There is no regular price for the mats. I take what I can get, and if we're very hard up I take very little. I get as little as 6d. and 4d. for each of the stitched mats, and as little as 1s. or 1s. 2d, for the rope mats. The last day I was out selling I went four miles into the country with four mats, three of the cheap sort and one of the best. I walked all day. Sold two and brought home two. I sold the dear one and one of the cheap ones, and had only 15d. for both. The time before that, I went out at seven in the morning, and never broke my fast. That day I sold three of the bag sort for 1s. 7d."

The woman in the next cellar hawks larger and superior mats in better neighbourhoods. She was a buxom dame from Sligo, with broad shoulders and a quick tongue. Her statement was to this effect: "I sell the

85

mats for as much as I can obtain. I have no fixed price. I ask as much as I think there is a chance of getting, and then bate. If I make a good day's sale in the morning I sell cheaper in the afternoon. Sometimes we're very poor and have only a little bread and coffee; but sometimes, when we're in good luck, we want for nothing. It all depends on the chance of sale. One day last week I walked to Tadcaster with mats. It is fourteen miles there and fourteen miles back. I took six mats with me, and sold five. They came, one with the other, to 5s. The highest price I can ever get for a rope mat is about 2s. or 2s. 4d. The sacking mats may fetch 6d, a piece."

In answer to further inquiries about the sacking which they used, I was told that the main part of it came from India, containing sugar. I observed that it seemed very clean. "Oh, indeed, sir," said the woman, "and it's well it may be clean. Sure they mashes it about and boils it before we get it, to take out the sweet stuff, to make treacle of. Sure, and it's few people would eat treacle if they knew what a deal of it came out of. I used to like a sup of it in my tay, but I'm cured of that now, anyhow."

I visited several cellars and wretched dwellings in the vicinity, inhabited by the Irish and the lowest class of English labourers, male and female, many of whom were engaged in the miserable occupation of unpicking old ropes, so as to prepare the oakum for being ground up again and wrought into shoddy, canvas and sacking. This species of labour is so unutterably wretched that it can only exist as eking out the pittance procured by the industry of the principal supports of the family.

The first woman upon whom I lighted, and who professed to follow this miserable trade, I found ill in bed. It was indeed a squalid household - the floor, dirty stone - the mean furniture, scanty and broken - the smashed window panes stuffed with rags -and an emaciated woman, ghastly as death, lying shivering on a flock bed on the floor, covered principally with a dress and a faded shawl. She told me that she could earn just 4d. by unpicking a stone of ordinary ropes, and that she was too weak to pick more than three stones a week. The family lived principally on parish relief. She did not mean to say that a better hand than she was could not make more by opening ropes. She could not work at it longer than from eight o'clock in the morning until four o'clock in the afternoon. It was a terribly dusty work. The house would be all covered with dust. The labour was awfully hard upon the fingers, particularly when the ropes were "green". For this kind of work, however, she was paid a penny a stone additional.

I was anxious to see the process actually going on, and presently 1 came upon a household in which, poor as were its physical attributes, the moral debasement and apathy which it disclosed were still more terrible. In a bare, stone-paved room, a principal part of the furniture of which consisted of tubs and apparatus for washing, sat three young children cowering over a spark of fire, and slowly and painfully tearing tough ropes to pieces with their weak, bony, little fingers. An intelligent girl, about eight or nine years of age, seemed to have the control of the other children, who were younger, and for whom she spoke, labouring away all the time. I ought to observe that I was accompanied by a relieving officer, and that the father of the family had been receiving parish relief for seven years:

"Where's your mother?" - "Gone out to try to get some washing to do."

"Where's your father?" - "In the Fleece - that's a public-house. Ah, mother told him he had better not go today, for you (to the relieving officer) would be very likely to come round, but he wouldn't stay."

"What does your father do?" - "Sweeps the streets, sometimes."

"But does not he help you to pick these ropes?" - "No; he wouldn't do that. He makes us do that."

"What do you get for picking? " - "Fourpence a stone, but I give it all to my mother."

"Do you go to school?" - "Only on Sundays. I must work you know. I can't read yet. But my little brother goes to school on week-days. Parson pays for him, only sometimes they keeps him at home to help in picking. He can't read either."

"And is not the other little boy your brother?" - Oh, no; he only comes in to help us to pick."

"Do you like picking?" - "No, because it makes me poorly. The dust gets into my eyes and down my throat, and makes me cough. Sometimes, too, it makes me sick. I can't keep at the work very long at a time because of that."

"You say you give all you earn to your mother, does she never let you have a penny for yourself?"

The poor child hung down her head, hesitated, and then stammered out -" Sometimes."

"And what do you do with it?" - "I buys bread."

In another house, very close to the last, I found three children left alone, but in idleness. The place was a mass of filth. The scanty furniture, broken and flung carelessly about - the unmade bed a chaos of brown rags – cracked and handleless cups, smeared with coffee grounds, on the floor - amid unemptied slops, and besides a large brown dish full of fermenting dough, upon which dust and ashes were rapidly settling as it stood at the fireside. The uncleaned window and the dim light of a winter's afternoon made the place so dark, that it was with difficulty I made out these details. There were here three little savages of children - their hair, tangled in filth-clotted masses, hanging over their grimy faces. Their clothes were mere bunches of rags, kept together by strings. A wriggle of their shoulders, and they would be free from all such incumbrances in a moment.

I asked them if they ever went to school? - "Never."

"Can you tell your letters?" - A mere stolid stare of ignorance.

"How old are you?" I asked the eldest girl. - "Don't know."

"Do you know what is the Queen's name?" -"No."

"Did you ever hear of anybody called the Queen?"-" No."

"Where were you born?" - "Don't know."

The relieving officer said he believed all the family were Irish.

"Did you ever hear of a place called Ireland?" - "No."

"Or of a place called England?" - "No."

"Or of a place called Yorkshire?" - "No."

"Do you know the name of this town?"

After a pause, this question was answered. The eldest girl did know that she lived in Leeds; and this knowledge, with the exception of matters belonging to the daily routine of existence, seemed positively to be the only piece of information in the possession of the family.

In two other houses, in both of which the inmates were receiving parish relief, the ignorance was almost equal. None of the children knew the Queen's name.

In each of these instances I must observe that the reason of the families being upon the parish was simply a temporary stoppage of the husband's employment in a mill. In neither case could the mother read. The relieving officer who was with me spoke of the improvident habits common among the Leeds operatives. A man who had been earning 20s. a week in a cloth mill for very many years, and had only his wife to support, came recently upon the parish ten days after he had been out of work. The officer said he knew of many similar cases.

I was struck during the course of my rambles in the Irish quarters of Leeds at the frequency with which pictures of the "Liberator" hung upon the walls.[1] Wherever the cottage or the cellar was filthiest and meanest - where potatoes to be eaten and rags to be picked lay mingled upon the floor - the features of Mr. O'Connell looked blandly down upon the squalor; and, in one or two instances, I found his effigy - supported by a repeal map of Ireland - the south and west coloured a vivid green, and the "Black North" tinted to a sable corresponding with the title.

A number of the cases of poverty which I was taken to see were those of wives with four or five children, deserted by their husbands. Others were the sad ones of old working men who had outlived their capability for labour. One of these individuals lived

---

[1] Daniel O'Connell (1775-1847), the Irish politician and patriot.

certainly in the blankest poverty I ever saw. In his room there was a bed, not worth, I should suppose, eighteenpence as old rags, and one solitary broken chair. The floor was sinking, and the laths showed in great patches, plasterless and bare. The occupant was an unshorn, little old man. He said, "I have nothing to do. I want to work, but they say I am too old. The parish pays 1s. a week for the rent of this room. I live on bread and water."

"Then why did you leave the workhouse?" said the relieving officer.

"Because I wanted my freedom," said the old man sitting down on his one broken chair. The sentiment must have been strong, to survive amid such misery. He had been a weaver, but had not flung a shuttle for near a dozen years. He had walked well nigh through Yorkshire trying for work, and had got none. Since he had been out of employment as a weaver, he had been a bricklayer's labour, and had earned as much as 17s. a week. but now he was too old for that, too old for anything. But he would not go into the house. No; he would have his freedom, and his bread and cold water. Another man, who would be in a similar position were it not for the kindness of his family, observed to me, "They say I'm past work. I'm not. I could work yet - only a little perhaps - but I could work. But things have come to that pass in this land, that lads and lasses have men's work."

The wages of hand-loom weavers in the woollen and worsted districts have puzzled, and do still puzzle me, sorely. I doubt not that the reader has often noted many apparent contradictions, or at all events very great variations, in the amounts stated as realised. But the truth is that, as I cannot generalise from contradictions, I am obliged sometimes to report contradictions.

In the course of one day's inquiry at Leeds I have had at least a dozen sums stated to me, by a dozen weavers, as a fair average of the weekly gains of their craft. The working foreman of the loom-shed noticed in my last letter, said that every industrious weaver could eat meat daily. Since then I have been again and again assured that if a hard-working weaver got porridge he might think himself well off. One man will tell you that he can hardly earn 6s. a week; another, in the next street, and weaving much the same sort of goods, will put down his gains as twice that sum. Here you will find a workman denouncing the power-loom as the cause of universal distress. His neighbour will probably opine that as much can be made by the weavers who tent the power-loom as could be earned by a workman fabricating by hand the coarse stuffs which the power-loom commonly makes, even if the machine in question had no existence.

No later than yesterday, a gentleman, who possesses an intimate acquaintance with operative life in Leeds, told me that 15s. was, in his belief, the very highest sum which the best weaver could clear at the best work. The very next house we entered, the workman stated that he commonly earned 17s. and 18s. per week.

The fact seems to be that there is an endless variety of prices paid for different sorts of goods - an endless variety in shades of industry and skill - and an endless variety of temperaments, inclining men to make the very best or the very worst of their cases.

In the cotton trade, the power-loom of course reigns supreme. In the stuff trade it is largely, but not, by any means, exclusively employed. In the woollen trade it plays a very subordinate part; and in both manufactures, as a general rule, it makes those kinds of fabrics for which the worst price would be paid were they wrought by hand.

It is really a puzzling case, when the weaver says pitifully, "Twenty years ago a man could make 26s. a week at this work, and now he can only make 8s." to go into the next street and there to find a workman engaged on what appears to be the same stuff, or at all events is very similar, and who avows that he is actually earning the alleged wages of twenty years ago.

That the average wages of weavers of all kinds - cotton hand-loom weaving I reckon as extinct - have greatly fallen, there can be doubt; but the standard from which they have sunk, and by which they are judged, is almost always the high one of the war prices.

It is commonly known that wages in England in 1810 were at least double the amount of wages in 1790. But poverty and toil appear to be in their nature fearfully chronic and immoveable. Two hundred years ago it would seem as if the cry of the hand-loom weavers was precisely what it is now. Even then the workmen complained that the good days of high pay were gone, and that modern masters and modern competition were grinding the faces of the poor. Mr. Macaulay quotes some verses of a song which was sung about the streets of Leeds in the reign of Charles II. *Mutatis mutandis*, the same burden yet rings mournfully in our ears. The popular poet represents the master clothier of Leeds speaking as follows:

"In former ages we used to give,
So that our work folks like farmers did live.

But the times are changed, we will make them to
know,
We will make them work hard for six pence a day,
Though a shilling they deserve if they had their
just pay,
If at all they murmur, and say 'tis too small,
We bid them choose whether they'll work at all.
And thus do we gain all our wealth and estate,
 By many poor men that work early and late,
Then hey for the clothing trade."

Such were the plaints of labour nearly two
centuries ago. It is sad and solemn to think that on the
very day preceding this on which I write, I heard men of
the same craft, working in the same place, utter the same
complaint - raising the old cry against the hardship of a
lot, which, as one labourer feelingly said to me, "makes a
man work like a slave, but don't allow him to live so well
as a slave."

The number of women in Leeds, and in other
manufacturing towns of all sorts, who make their living
by their needles, is very small. The work of the mill is far
shorter and easier than that of the sempstress; and in the
case of the few who do ply the needle, the vicinage of the
mills keeps their wages somewhat above that starvation
point below which they have elsewhere sunk. I
discovered, however, one most miserable case. The
woman in question had been a stay-stitcher working at
the lowest and coarsest sort or stays - generally small
brown ones for children. When I saw her she was ill in
bed - a white, ghastly looking creature. Three people
lived in the room beside herself - a decrepit father and
mother, and a grown-up brother fast dying of

consumption. The stay-stitcher occupied the only bed in the room. It was of that miserable sort I have so often described, and there was another similar couch spread on the floor in a corner.

The little strip of carpet on the dirty floor was as ragged as a net; the poor half-broken furniture, and cooking and eating utensils, such as they were, lay scattered about in that strange disorder which I have learnt to believe does not always indicate slovenliness, but the disregard and carelessness engendered by utter and abject misery. The small window was fast closed against the cold, and in consequence the air was foul and stifling.

The woman told me that she had been paid for stitching stays, 4d., 6d., and 8d. a pair, according to their size. But there was little more work in the largest than in the smallest kind, although the price was double. To make a pair of small ones took her a long day's work. Often and often she had kept at it till twelve at night. Some weeks she made 3s., some weeks 4s.

She did not, however, intend to resume the trade when she recovered. She intended to take in shoe binding. She could only do the slippers, however - particularly carpet slippers. The prices were 1d. per pair, and it would take her a hard day's work to finish half a dozen pair. She did not understand mill work. Of course this family were mainly supported by the parish, from which they drew about 6s. a week.

Shoe binding is better paid than slipper binding - the work required being neater, and demanding more skill. One woman, a binder, whom I questioned, worked at low-priced shoes. She was only paid 15d. a dozen; and she calculated that she could make 8s. a day, if she were fully employed. This woman had four children - one by her husband, who had been transported, and three by another man since that event. The parish gave her 1s. 6d. per head per week.

Not far from this person I found another shoe-binder, employed on the best sort of work. Here was a tolerably comfortable home. The husband and wife sat on each side of the fire plying their tasks. He made shoes for one master, and she bound shoes for another. She was paid sometimes 2s. 6d., sometimes 3s., sometimes 3s. 6d. per dozen, and she could earn in "good weeks" about 6s. or 7s. She found her own silk and thread, and had constant work.

I visited the only two slop-workers I could hear of. One was receiving public charity, the other was the wife of a weaver, who stated that he earned 17s. a week. The former made in substance the following statement:

She laboured at fustian and corduroy trowsers, working-jackets, and working-sleeved waistcoats. All these garments were lined with cotton. For making a pair of trowsers she had 10d. and her thread found her. She could make a pair in a day By a day she meant from seven in the morning till ten o'clock at night.

For lined jackets and sleeved waistcoats she used to get 15d. each, but the price had been reduced lately.

Sometimes she made drawers, for which she was paid 4d. a pair. They had buttons and button holes all complete.

Work as she might, she could not finish two pair in a day, and the utmost she could make in a week, with the very hardest labour, was 5s.

The second slopworker was principally employed upon boys' dresses. These she made of three sorts and sizes. The first, and smallest size, consisted of a jacket and trowsers, the latter buttoning over the former. For such a suit, generally of corduroy, she received 1s. 4d., and she could make one in a day.

The second-class suit consisted of a jacket, waistcoat, and trowsers. For this she was paid 2s. 6d., and to make it took a good day and a half.

The third-class suit consisted of a surtout with skirts, a waistcoat, and a jacket. For this she was paid 3s. 6d., and she took more than two days to earn it.

These were the main articles of dress, which she sewed, and she cut them out herself. She sometimes, however, made moleskin jackets and waistcoats, such as are worn by engineers. These, from the nature of the stuff, are very hard work. For a waistcoat of this kind, with sleeves, she was paid 1s. 3d. For a double-breasted waistcoat, without sleeves, she was paid 9d.

Her hours of work were from seven in the morning until ten, eleven, or twelve o'clock, as the case might be. She found her own thread. In all the garments which she made she put regular lining.

In the course of my wanderings through Leeds, I encountered two or three women engaged in a rather curious trade, a description of which I am not able to give with technical accuracy, though I can easily make clear the object in view. Like most occupations, the cloth trade has its share of tricks, one of which consists in passing off an inferior for a superior kind of cloth by some legerdemain practised in the dyeing process. The deception, were it not for the ingenious device I saw being practised, would, however, I was told, be exposed at once by the peculiar action of the dye employed upon the selvage of the cloth. The object, therefore, is to dye the cloth without dyeing the selvage upon its borders, and for the purpose the piece is delivered to a woman, who "selves" it - that is to say, who rolls up the selvage into a circular cylinder all round the cloth, and then covers it with a sort of envelope, tightly stitched and perfectly water-proof. The whole is then plunged into the dye-vat, and after being duly taken out and dried the sewing is unpicked, and the selvage unrolled precisely in its original state.

The women employed in this adroit trickery have about 10d. per piece for sewing up the selvage, and 2d. per piece for unpicking it after the cloth comes from the dyers' hands. A good work-woman will earn from 5s. to 6s. a week, but the work is seldom regular. One of the women engaged in it had been "playing" for three weeks before she got the piece upon which I found her labouring. The parish, of course, is in the meantime supporting her and her sick child.

The Leeds Mechanics' Institution[1] is a prosperous and vigorous working establishment. It counts four life members, 143 proprietary members, 379 subscribers, at 15s. yearly, 455 at 12s., and 583 members paying 10s., 8s., and 5s., annually. The number of day scholars is 94, and the mutual improvement class includes 210 - making a total of 1,868 members. The statistics of this Institution are collected with more ease than is at all usual in similar establishments, and I am, therefore, enabled to present some interesting general results.

For the last year the number of pupils entered in the arithmetic and mensuration class has been 35 - average attendance, 22; writing and book-keeping 34 -

---

[1] In South Parade. The Institution was founded in 1824 and merged with the Literary Institution in 1842.

average attendance 23; grammar and geography, 14 - attendance 11; drawing, 45 - attendance, 30; analytical chemistry, 11 - attendance, 9; manufacturing chemistry, 4 - attendance, 4; French evening class, 17 - attendance, 12; ditto ladies', 4 - attendance, 4; German class, 9 - attendance, 9.

The library contains 7,028 volumes. The issue of books in the past year, including periodicals, make a total of 57,174 volumes. These issues. with reference to the species of works in demand, are classed as follows:

Books on theology, were given out 1,784 times; on philosophy and education, 3,089 times; on politics and statistics, 572 times; on history and biography, 9,129 times; on voyages and travels, 3,074 times; poetry and the drama, 1,887 times; works of fiction, 15,675 times; fine arts and literature, 4,450; mathematics, 483; mechanics, 651; chemistry, 997; natural philosophy, 995; medicine and dietetics, 533; bound periodicals, 4,926; foreign works, 172; unbound periodicals, 8,256 - making a grand total of 57.174.

The features which may be noted in this return are - the great demand for works of fiction, and the small demand for works of any character in any language save English.

The total number of lectures delivered last year was 39. They embrace a wide range of subjects - literary, historic, economic, scientific, and artistic.

In connection with the institute there is a school of design, attended by an average of 11 male and 13 female pupils in the morning, and 30 male pupils at night.

The annual Government grant to this school has lately been raised from £80 to £150, in addition to which some ninety volumes of works connected with the arts have been sent down by the Council of the Government School of Design, to form the nucleus of an Art library.

It is quite impossible to overrate the importance of these seminaries throughout the manufacturing districts. In every respect, save the single one of drawing patterns, our manufacturing population seem to carry all before them. The industrial spirit is abroad in its strength, but the art-spirit is weak and cold. It was humiliating in the calico districts to see the abject dependence of English manufacturers upon French pattern designers. In too many instances a notion seemed to prevail that to invent beautiful and tasteful forms was the province of the French, while to stamp them upon cotton cloth was the business of the English. It is to be hoped that the influence of the numerous Schools of Design now springing up in the North may tend in some degree to counteract that hard-headed contempt for everything but what is exclusively practical and "businesslike," which stamps so uninviting an impression upon the surface aspect of the manufacturing system.

The Leeds Mechanics' Institution is at present some four hundred pounds in debt; but a series of exhibitions and explanations, by Mr. Frederick Warren, the well-known lecturer upon the cotton trade, of his working models, which is about to take place on behalf of the institution, will, it is hoped, remove the greater portion of its liabilities.

Before leaving the manufacturing districts, it may not be amiss that I should devote a few words to the life and toil of the men, who, before the era of railroads, were chiefly concerned in the conveyance of heavy goods from place to place, and who still transport by water-carriage a very considerable proportion of our manufactured and mineral wealth - I mean the bargemen engaged in navigating our inland canals.

The railway passenger will be familiar with the aspect of these men and their boats. The canal and the rail often run together for many a mile, each crossing the other in its windings. Thus, as the train puffs across the viaduct, the passenger may often mark the shining course of the canal, glittering in its long serpentine undulations beneath him, the unruffled clayey water, the mud-trampled towing-path, and the green meadows sloping on either hand to the brink with here and there a fringe of willows or rushy plants rising from the water.

Gliding along these tranquil channels come barges, which, creeping slowly but surely along, make their gradual way from Lancashire to Surrey, and from the Thames to the Severn.

The boats are long, narrow, and deeply laden. A tarpaulin covers the cargo stowed amidships; and sometimes in the bow, sometimes in the stern, sometimes in both bow and stern, rise one or two funnels - the number being according to the size of the boat - smoking cheerily, and proclaiming that the cabins of captain and crew lie beneath.

As a general rule, a single horse draws these boats along, the driver being frequently seated complacently upon its back, with both feet towards the water. This individual belongs to a class often talked of but seldom seen. In the slang of the canals he is called the "Horse Marine". The "marine" is, indeed, his regular trade appellation.

Sometimes a man, or a couple of men, lounge idly on the barge's deck - occasionally a woman taking a "trick" at the helm is the only person visible.

Let us descend into the after cabin of one of the larger class of barges - one carrying from forty to fifty tons. It is a hot, choky, little box, between four and five feet high; near the scuttle is a stove. On either side run berths made after the usual fashion afloat. One is very generally constructed broad enough to contain a couple of persons; the other has often only room for one. Beneath them are lockers which serve for seats, and at the stern, just forward of the rudder, opens the little cupboard, wherein the "sea stock" is deposited.

Even with the scuttle open you will probably find the air close and oppressive, but the captain will generally tell you that two, sometimes three, people sleep there with the hatch on: "We move it so as to make a chink if we feel it over hot."

The larger boats are generally navigated by a captain and two "mates", and helped, of course, by the "marine". The average wages of the captain amount to about 22s.- those of the mates and the marine to 18s. weekly. The captain has often his wife on board, but sometimes one of the mates give his "missus" a trip, the skipper on these occasions gallantly giving up the use of the cabin and sleeping with the other mate in the forecastle. Only one lady, however, is allowed to be on board at a time.

The usual speed of the barges is from two to three miles and a half an hour. The "fly" barges, which are commonly the larger sort, proceed night and day, never stopping, except at the locks, and to deliver goods. Each horse performs a stage of from twenty to twenty-five miles. The marine in charge of the relay knows when the barge will be up, "to an hour or two" - a latitude reminding one of the very old coaching days. The smaller barges have only a single horse, which goes the whole journey.

These boats "tie up" at nights. The bargemen always sleep on board. The marine looks after his steed, and sleeps ashore. There do not seem to be any regular watches on board these barges, as at sea. The turns of duty depend upon circumstances and varying arrangements. Three hours is reckoned a fair spell at the helm, and if there is a woman on board she always steers when the men are at their dinners. In passing a lock, however, all hands must be on deck, by day or night. The foregoing sketch would seem to indicate that the inland bargemen lead a life of comparative comfort.

Printed in the United Kingdom
by Lightning Source UK Ltd.
128261UK00001B/100-198/A